Quality and Equity
of Schooling in Scotland

OECD

ORGANISATION FOR ECONOMIC CO-OPERATION AND DEVELOPMENT

The OECD is a unique forum where the governments of 30 democracies work together to address the economic, social and environmental challenges of globalisation. The OECD is also at the forefront of efforts to understand and to help governments respond to new developments and concerns, such as corporate governance, the information economy and the challenges of an ageing population. The Organisation provides a setting where governments can compare policy experiences, seek answers to common problems, identify good practice and work to co-ordinate domestic and international policies.

The OECD member countries are: Australia, Austria, Belgium, Canada, the Czech Republic, Denmark, Finland, France, Germany, Greece, Hungary, Iceland, Ireland, Italy, Japan, Korea, Luxembourg, Mexico, the Netherlands, New Zealand, Norway, Poland, Portugal, the Slovak Republic, Spain, Sweden, Switzerland, Turkey, the United Kingdom and the United States. The Commission of the European Communities takes part in the work of the OECD.

OECD Publishing disseminates widely the results of the Organisation's statistics gathering and research on economic, social and environmental issues, as well as the conventions, guidelines and standards agreed by its members.

This work is published on the responsibility of the Secretary-General of the OECD. The opinions expressed and arguments employed herein do not necessarily reflect the official views of the Organisation or of the governments of its member countries.

Also available in French under the title:
Examens des politiques nationales d'éducation
Qualité et équité de l'enseignement scolaire en Écosse

Reprinted 2008

Corrigenda to OECD publications may be found on line at: *www.oecd.org/publishing/corrigenda*.

© OECD 2007

Foreword

Reviews of National Policies for Education are a mainstay of the OECD's efforts to draw on international experience and to give countries advice on how to strengthen education. However, the nature of these reviews has changed in important ways with the increased importance attached to education policy, and the greater availability of information on education systems and more robust evidence of their performance.

This review of the quality and equity of the outcomes of school education in Scotland was undertaken to examine the strengths of Scotland's schools and offer advice on how to meet the challenges they face in securing high standards for all children. It marks an important step forward in the Organisation's efforts to further interpret country-specific results from the Programme for International Student Assessment (PISA) and to draw implications for policy. It also further strengthens the comparative framework within which the Organisation conducts its peer reviews of national policies for education. This review benchmarks important aspects of Scottish performance against performance of several other countries whose size and circumstances are such that they are useful 'comparators'. The team of independent examiners who carried out this review further reinforce efforts to strengthen the framework for comparative analysis: the examiners come from four of the 'comparator' countries; they know their own systems well and have valuable insights into the policy and institutional arrangements that drive performance.

In their report the examiners describe the strong overall performance of Scottish school education. The examiners express concern over achievement gaps that appear in primary education and uneven participation and completion patterns in secondary education. They make 18 recommendations on how these challenges might be met. They praise the high degree of dedication and proficiency of professionals in the system, the commitment of the Government to spur improvement, and the capacity of local authorities and schools to implement needed reforms.

On 11 December 2007 the OECD Education Policy Committee and the Scottish Government will discuss the findings and recommendations of the review. It then will become part of the public debate of education reform in Scotland. Its ultimate value will hinge on how well it nourishes that debate and how the Scottish Government interprets and applies its messages. I look forward to the outcome of this process. The Scottish Government has demonstrated great openness to outside examination, and commitment to looking beyond its borders for examples of good policy and practice.

This report was prepared by Richard V. Teese of Australia, rapporteur and chair, and Simo Juva of Finland, Frances Kelly of New Zealand, and Dirk Van Damme of Belgium. Gregory Wurzburg, Karin Zimmer, Deborah Fernandez and Sabrina Leonarduzzi of the OECD Secretariat supported the work of the examiners.

A background report, *OECD Review of the Quality and Equity of Education Outcomes in Scotland: Diagnostic Report,* was prepared by the Scottish Government and is available on the OECD website http://dx.doi.org/10.1787/148012367602 www.oecd.org/edu/reviews/nationalpolicies.

Barbara Ischinger, Director for Education
Organisation for Economic Co-operation and Development
December 2007

Acknowledgements

The authors of this report wish to acknowledge the kind assistance of Tim Simons, Jeff Maguire, Joanna Mackenzie, Pete Whitehouse, and Bill Maxwell from the Scottish Government, and are very grateful for the guidance and support offered by Gregory Wurzburg, Karin Zimmer and Deborah Fernandez from the OECD Secretariat, and for editorial assistance from Nicky Dulfer of the Centre for Post-Compulsory Education and Lifelong Learning in the University of Melbourne.

Table of contents

List of Figures

Executive Summary

In 2006 the Scottish education authorities asked the OECD to examine in depth the performance of the school system within the framework of the Organisation's reviews of national policies for education. The purpose of the review was to examine the strengths of Scotland's schools and the challenges they face in securing high standards for all children. The Scottish authorities were particularly interested in receiving advice about the adequacy of recent reforms in view of the experience of several 'comparator countries' facing similar challenges. After the Scottish Government and the OECD Secretariat agreed on Terms of Reference to guide such a review, the Secretariat assembled a team of independent examiners with extensive experience in four of the comparator countries identified by the Scottish Government. The Scottish Government, in consultation with the OECD Secretariat, prepared a Background Report—*OECD Review of the Quality and Equity of Education Outcomes in Scotland: Diagnostic Report* (SEED 2007)[1]—to provide the examiners with an overview of the Scottish Education system. The examiners visited Scotland early in 2007.

The report of the examiners takes an international perspective in assessing how well Scottish schools perform and examines both PISA findings and national test and examinations results in the context of educational reform, both within Scotland and without. This executive summary offers only a brief overview of strengths. These are very fully explored in Chapter 2 of the report. The challenges receive more detailed attention in this summary, as a discussion of these is essential for setting the context of the review's recommendations. Chapter 1 explains how this report is organized as well as giving more background to the OECD review. Terms of reference are reproduced in Annex 1.

---

[1] In September 2007 Scottish Ministers formally adopted the title Scottish Government to replace the term Scottish Executive as an expression of corporate identity. For more details, see: http://www.scotland.gov.uk/News/Releases/2007/09/31160110

Strengths

Scotland performs at a consistently very high standard in the Programme for International Student Assessment (PISA). Few countries can be said with confidence to outperform it in mathematics, reading and science. Scotland also has one of the most equitable school systems in the OECD. Only a very small proportion of Scottish 15 year-olds are assessed in the lowest bands of performance. Headteachers are amongst the most positive of school principals in the OECD in judging the adequacy of staffing and teaching resources, and students are generally very positive about their schools. Underpinning the impressive international performance of Scottish schools is a system of near-universal and high-quality pre-school education.

On national tests, many children are one or two years in advance of expected levels. There have been significant reductions in under-achievement. There is now greater consistency of achievement in the earlier years of primary school. Higher proportions of students in the final year of compulsory school are passing at the highest levels of the examinations. Notable progress has been made in improving the achievement of children living in poverty.

The OECD examiners were impressed by the capacity of Scottish primary schools to respond to public expectations of continuously improving standards and consistency of outcomes. This is in a context in which Scotland depends more than ever on the quality and impact of its schools. Indicators of improvement as well as high international standards also show that Scotland's confidence in its comprehensive system of secondary schools is well-placed.

Publicly-funded school education is the responsibility of Scottish local authorities. It is through them that an equitable distribution of resources across Scotland is managed, and they are also responsible for ensuring that schools are responsive to community needs, adaptive, and effective. The community assets represented by schools are in capable hands. The professionalism and commitment of the education departments of the local authorities makes wider reliance on them a good strategy.

Scotland has been a leader in testing the effectiveness of its schools and curriculum through student destinations monitoring. Continued commitment to transparency of outcomes for all of Scotland's young people, whoever they may be, matches the high level of trust placed in public schools. Coupled with this is a system of universal and individualised careers counselling.

Scotland has invested heavily in school education. The Teachers' Agreement (2001) has had a wide-ranging impact on teacher morale and on interest in the profession through substantial salary increases, improved working conditions, and continuous professional development. Scotland's approach to teacher induction is world class, and the Scottish Qualification for Headship is an outstanding and demanding programme. Renovation of schools is occurring through a major building and refurbishment programme.

Challenges

On the measures quoted above, Scotland is building a strong platform of achievement in basic education. One major challenge facing Scottish schools is to reduce the achievement gap that opens up about Primary 5 and continues to widen throughout the junior secondary years (S1 to S4). Children from poorer communities and low socio-economic status homes are more likely than others to under-achieve, while the gap associated with poverty and deprivation in local government areas appears to be very wide.

A second challenge relates to the need to build on the strong platform of basic education through socially broader and more successful participation in upper secondary education and greater equity in Scottish higher education. Inequalities in staying-on rates, participation at different academic levels of national courses, and pass rates in these courses are a concern. So, too, are the number of young people leaving school with minimal (and in some cases no) qualifications and the comparatively high proportion in precarious transition.

Understanding the challenges

To respond well to these challenges hinges on having a good understanding of the causes of under-achievement. PISA findings provide valuable insights. Little of the variation in student achievement in Scotland is associated with the ways in which schools differ. Most of it is connected with how children differ. Who you are in Scotland is far more important than what school you attend, so far as achievement differences on international tests are concerned. Socio-economic status is the most important difference between individuals. Family cultural capital, life-style, and aspirations influence student outcomes through the nature of the cognitive and cultural demands of the curriculum, teacher values, the programme emphasis in schools, and peer effects.

That differences between schools contribute relatively little variation in student achievement highlights the importance of cultural and organisational factors which are common to Scottish schools, but which weigh unequally on individuals from different family backgrounds. National attainment data confirm the point-in-time picture from PISA that children from poorer homes are more likely to under-achieve, disengage from schoolwork, leave school earlier than others, and—if they continue—study at lower academic levels and record lower pass rates. The geographical perspective that national data afford also show that deprivation intensifies the effects of family socio-economic status and of a predominantly academic culture in schools through the concentration of multiple disadvantages in schools serving poor communities.

While there is no formal prescription of the curriculum, innovation appears to be modest (as confirmed by the National Debate on curriculum in 2002), and schools have only limited flexibility in teaching resources. These are the two key instruments of change and adaptation in schools. So lack of more freedom in them makes achieving high standards for all groups of students more difficult.

Schools should be able to build the mix of staffing they need to tackle the particular challenges they face and to offer programmes which best address these challenges. Greater management freedom in these two areas needs to be part of a compact with local government which establishes expectations in exchange for autonomy, and encourages and protects innovation and risk-taking through an authoritative mandate.

Addressing the challenges

A new curriculum is on the way in Scotland. The OECD review was impressed by the breadth of vision and commitment to both high standards and social inclusiveness in the concept documents of a Curriculum for Excellence as well as in the wide consultation process. Earlier reforms of curriculum and examinations in Scotland succeeded in expanding social access to secondary education. But they did so by differentiating levels of cognitive demand to reduce academic barriers. With higher levels of staying-on now achieved, the national goal is to raise standards of achievement—that is, to increase demands on students. This is reflected in the defined purposes of the new 3-18 curriculum.

To meet the goal of successfully raising demands on students can only be done by building strong incentives into study programmes. Intrinsic incentives relate to quality of teaching, enjoyment of learning, robust instructional design, formative assessment, continuous feedback, individual attention, and sensitivity to student learning style. Extrinsic incentives relate to the economic benefits of school. They include skills, generic and specific competencies, practical experience, access to accredited vocational training, and good pathways to further education, training, and employment.

A Curriculum for Excellence aims to deepen and enrich the demands made on students. A learner perspective on what counts as enjoyable and valuable learning is therefore essential. International experience suggests that Scotland would gain from a bolder, but also broader approach to vocational studies in schools than it has so far demonstrated. Vocational education and training should not be seen too narrowly in terms of employability.

In this report, we consider vocational studies to involve a mix of courses which place an emphasis on applied and collaborative learning, problem-solving, sharing of learning tasks, overt meaning and purpose, formative and competency-based assessment, and real-world orientation. Vocational studies are intended to form the whole person and to be motivational and constructive of broad capacities. However, their economic rationale is important, should be explicit, and must involve proven quality of training.

Progressing the new 3-18 curriculum presents a major challenge to Scottish authorities. Incentive-building must be a major part of addressing the challenge. But to deliver on the incentives will require much greater freedom in curriculum both for local authorities and for schools themselves. Flexibility cannot reside simply in broad study designs or approved margins of freedom to vary time devoted to particular areas of the curriculum. Local authorities are well placed to determine the balance of learning opportunities that should be available to their communities, and schools need substantial freedom of action within a framework of agreed goals and outcomes to vary the courses they offer.

In Scotland, local government is responsible for the delivery of school education. The capacity of local councils to ensure a more consistent pattern of outcomes across Scotland is limited partly by funding arrangements and partly by inflexibility in national curricula and examinations. Local councils are the main vehicle of redistributive funding to schools, but their capacity to address relative need within their boundaries is not necessarily enhanced by direct "ring-fenced" grants from government to schools, by multiple funding lines, complex accountability arrangements, and reverse "claw back" productivity transfers.

Local authorities have only limited influence over the curriculum in schools and over the full range of learning opportunities available to the communities they serve. Promotion of change in schools is hampered by the vulnerability of schools to adverse perceptions and judgements based on examination results. Although local authorities are the employers of teachers and the builders of schools, their influence is limited by wider arrangements which have a centralizing and conforming effect.

The OECD review considers that greater flexibility is needed in arrangements linking local councils to the Scottish Government, and linking schools in turn to local government. But without greater flexibility in arrangements relating to curriculum, examinations, and qualifications, more autonomy for councils and schools will not go far.

At the same time, the OECD review is concerned that greater local council and school autonomy in matters of finance and curriculum needs to be counter-balanced by greater transparency and accountability. The Scottish Government does not have reliable information on the extent to which educational standards are being reached in each of the 32 local authorities. Information that is available points to very wide national variations in test scores and exam results. While this report notes significant improvements in student learning outcomes, there is a risk that greater autonomy could lead to greater variability.

To counter this possibility, policy instruments should be adopted which set down clear expectations about improvement in student opportunities and outcomes and are backed by a comprehensive survey and monitoring programme which furnishes reliable data to the Scottish Government, local authorities, and schools.

There is also a concern that without reliable data on student achievement and school performance throughout Scotland, the suitability and effectiveness of the current methodology for distributing grants to local authorities cannot be tested. The formula allocation of block grants—whose obscurity is not without attracting a certain pride—is weighted for deprivation, but this is an input-driven approach whose impact on differences in student achievement is unknown. As regional inequalities in Scotland appear to be both large and persistent, lack of knowledge about the effectiveness of national-to-local government financial arrangements is significant. There needs to be a more integrated approach, with the funding methodology tied to a national strategy, clear objectives, transparency, and regular assessment of impact.

Recommendations

To tackle the environment of poverty and deprivation and to renovate the way good schools routinely work, the OECD review suggests five broadly-framed strategies:

– **National priorities funding through local government compacts**

– **Greater school autonomy in a local government framework**

– **A comprehensive, structured, and accessible curriculum**

– **Continuous review of curriculum and teaching**

– **Monitoring of student destinations.**

These strategies aim at creating greater flexibility for the agencies which exercise the most direct responsibility for how well schools work. We have sought a balance between greater freedom of action, on the one hand, and greater transparency and accountability, on the other.

The first two strategies relate to the delivery system—how the national government gets money to local government (under a compact) and how local government puts resources into schools (again under a compact). The next three strategies are about defining, implementing and evaluating the programme of demands made on students (and on their teachers). These strategies concern the curriculum as a national framework, but also as it is delivered in the many varying sites across Scotland.

National priorities funding through, local government compacts

Recommendation 1. That the Scottish Government develops a national innovation plan to fund improvements in educational opportunities and outcomes through negotiated agreements with local authorities ("national innovation agreements").

Recommendation 2. That funding for the current Schools of Ambition programme be applied in a more selective and targeted way through the national innovation plan.

Recommendation 3. That the Scottish Survey of Achievement be extended to all children throughout Scotland as a basis for negotiating resource and outcome agreements with local authorities and to enable improvements in schools to be measured at an individual and sub-group level.

Greater school autonomy in a local government framework

Recommendation 4. That each local authority develops a policy framework which defines the priority impacts it seeks to make under the national innovation plan, including targeted improvements in student opportunities and outcomes.

Recommendation 5. That where a local authority provides additional resources to schools for equity purposes, it should do so within the framework of the national innovation plan as a means of concentrating the total resources available to a school, consolidating funds to achieve more flexibility and reliability, and enhancing the ability of the authority to evaluate programme effectiveness.

Recommendation 6. That local authorities negotiate agreements with schools under which greater management autonomy in staffing and curriculum is established in return for progress on an agreed platform of improvement in learning opportunities and outcomes.

A comprehensive, structured and accessible curriculum

Recommendation 7. That each local authority develop an explicit policy framework which contains a charter of learning opportunities—a commitment to provide a range of education and training places in a delivery configuration which best suits the circumstances and needs of its communities.

Recommendation 8. That, as a matter of national policy, vocational courses be accessible to all young people in schools from S3, and that sequences of study be developed spanning the compulsory and post-compulsory years.

Recommendation 9. That the Scottish Government support school-based provision of vocational courses where local authorities seek to implement this model within the framework of the national innovation plan.

Recommendation 10. That each local authority establish a curriculum planning and pathways network which links schools, colleges and employer groups to assist in establishing a charter of learning opportunities and defining the pathways through school to further education, training and employment.

Recommendation 11. That Standard Grades examinations be phased out as the new 3-18 curriculum is implemented and as clearer and more effective pathways are established for the whole range of young people.

Recommendation 12. That a Scottish Certificate of Education be developed to sanction completion of an approved programme of studies or training, whether in school, college or employment. This "graduation" certificate should have defined minimum requirements to reflect the purposes of the new 3-18 curriculum, but also substantial flexibility as to content, level and duration of studies to ensure accessibility.

Recommendation 13. That young people proceeding to S5 undertake a programme of studies with specified minimum standards leading to the award of a Scottish Certificate of Education at the end of that year or at the end of S6, depending on the individual study pattern.

Recommendation 14. That those young people who choose to leave at the end of compulsory school negotiate an individual plan for further education and training to be undertaken over the next two years under supervision of an appropriate authority (e.g., a college), and that, if specified minimum standards of achievement or competency are met, they be awarded a Scottish Certificate of Education.

Continuous review of curriculum and teaching

Recommendation 15. That education authorities in Scotland examine current approaches to gathering student feedback on quality of teaching (e.g., the Student Evaluation of Learning software) and that they work with teachers to gain wider acceptance of the most promising approaches.

Recommendation 16. That rolling consultations be undertaken with teachers from a wide cross-section of schools regarding their classroom experience in delivering selected courses, the quality of course design, and learning outcomes for students.

Monitoring school leaver destinations

Recommendation 17. That consideration be given to extending the scope of the Scottish Survey of School Leavers to make contact with young people well before they leave school and to provide fuller information about school achievement and experience.

Recommendation 18. That Careers Scotland investigate approaches to providing all schools and local authorities with comprehensive point-in-time data on school destinations, including work and study status, jobs, and hours of work, and broken out by qualification level and gender (at a minimum).

References

Scottish Executive Education Department (2007), *OECD Review of the Quality and Equity of Education Outcomes in Scotland: Diagnostic Report*, available on the OECD website http://dx.doi.org/10.1787/148012367602 or www.oecd.org/edu/reviews/nationalpolicies.

1. Introduction

Scope of the OECD review of Scottish school education

In November 2006, the Scottish Executive invited the OECD to conduct a review of quality and equity of education outcomes in Scotland. The purpose of the review was to compare the performance of Scottish education to that of other OECD countries. The review was seen as a means of assessing strengths and identifying challenges, and of exploring approaches which might add to the Scottish reform agenda in overcoming the challenges and further reinforcing strengths and improving performance.

The scope of the review is principally school education, and the transitions to and from this. Key areas of concern are the consistency of education outcomes across Scotland, equity of outcomes for young people from different social backgrounds and personal circumstances (*e.g.*, 'looked after' children, young people with additional support needs), and the performance of the lowest attaining young people relative to other learners. The review also looks at issues such as leadership, disengagement from learning, and transitions across sectors. It seeks to identify key levers for positive change in order to ensure that all young people are able to achieve their full potential.

The approach in this report is to draw on results from the Programme for International Student Assessment (PISA) to highlight strengths and to identify challenges, to draw extensively on national test and examinations data to look more closely at institutional arrangements and processes (such as curriculum and qualifications), and to set findings on post-school transition within the framework of projected labour market change in Scotland.

Where appropriate, the report makes reference to policy and practice in OECD comparator nations (and some others), and more generally examines the Scottish scene from international research perspectives. Extensive use has been made of Scottish educational research, statistical information, and policy documents.

Participation of Scotland in the review

The OECD team visited Scotland in March 2007 (details are set out in Annex 2). The aim was to meet teachers and headteachers from schools, directors and professional officers from local education authorities, and officials from a range of organisations, including the Scottish Executive Education Department (SEED), the Scottish Qualifications Authority (SQA), Learning and Teaching Scotland (LTS), the General Teaching Council for Scotland, and other bodies. In addition, the review team participated in a number of invitational seminars. All of these sessions proved to be very stimulating and informative, and gave the review team wide exposure to issues in Scottish education.

Key questions to be addressed in the review included:

a. Viewed from an international perspective, what are the strengths and weaknesses of education in Scotland, particularly with reference to those who are not achieving their full potential, including those at risk of becoming part of the Not in Education Employment or Training (NEET) group.

b. Do the range of current reforms, including specifically work in progress on the wider agenda of a Curriculum for Excellence, address the challenges sufficiently? How well do the reforms compare with reforms in countries which have common issues to deal with? How effective have implementation policies, particularly in respect of outcome-based curriculum reforms, been in comparator nations?

c. Are there international insights in the delivery of education to young people at risk of underachieving from which Scotland might draw? If so, what appear to be the principal benefits and advantages of these approaches to Scotland? And what are the most plausible strategies to deploy in a manner that respects the culture, values, and traditions of Scottish education?

d. How well do current reforms disseminate to the classroom? How effective are they at changing behaviour on the ground? Are the key messages being communicated effectively and getting through the system?

e. How sustainable is the current direction of travel?

To address these questions, the review team was assisted by a Diagnostic Report prepared by SEED (SEED, 2007). At the conclusion of the March visit, the review team presented initial impressions to a well-attended seminar, organized by the Department.

Extensive research and analysis were subsequently conducted, with the help of documentary and statistical material gathered during the March visit or supplied later by SEED. The review wishes to thank Tim Simons, Jeff Maguire, Joanna Mackenzie, Pete Whitehouse, and Bill Maxwell. Their help, and that of many other officers, has greatly contributed to the performance of this review.

Structure of this report

The purpose of this report is to examine the strengths of Scottish school education, to identify the challenges, and to indicate potentially fruitful lines of action, building on policies and initiatives that are currently being implemented, either in Scotland itself or in its comparator nations.

Strengths are examined in Chapter 2. This is a wide-ranging and not uncritical examination. It is important to highlight those aspects of Scottish school education that provide the framework for further improvement, while noting areas where potential is not being met.

The international evidence of the comparative performance of Scottish schools is presented in Chapter 3. Scotland performs highly on overall achievement in PISA and also on equity. But beyond the now well-known rankings, what do PISA findings reveal about the consistency of student outcomes in Scotland and the factors affecting equity?

In Chapter 4, national test and examinations data are drawn on to help identify the processes and factors which contribute to unevenness in the performance of a school system that ranks high on multiple international measures. The aim in this chapter is to prepare the ground for a later discussion of intervention policies and strategies.

A concern for 'who gets what?' also runs through Chapter 5, whose focus is on school staying-on rates and transition from school to work or further education and training. This chapter sets the scene by presenting the directions of economic and labour market change in Scotland.

Chapter 6 offers a review of Scotland's curriculum reform efforts, including *A Curriculum for Excellence* and Skills for Work programmes. Chapter 7 builds on this review and offers a set of recommendations for change. The analysis and the recommendations are set within a framework of two main strategies for improvement which build on or augment existing policies and initiatives.

The main author of this report was the rapporteur, Richard Teese. The other examiners on the team were Simo Juva (Finland), Frances Kelly (New Zealand), and Dirk Van Damme (Flemish Community of Belgium), who contributed to the writing. The team as a whole take responsibility for the final product. The authors are very grateful for the guidance and support offered by Gregory Wurzburg, Karin Zimmer and Deborah Fernandez from the OECD Secretariat, and to Nicky Dulfer of CPELL, the University of Melbourne, for editorial assistance.

References

Scottish Executive Education Department (2007), *OECD Review of the Quality and Equity of Education Outcomes in Scotland: Diagnostic Report*, available on the OECD website http://dx.doi.org/10.1787/148012367602 or www.oecd.org/edu/reviews/nationalpolicies.

2. Strengths of Scottish School Education

Scottish school education—a brief overview

Scotland is a well-schooled nation by international standards. Nearly 60% of the working age population have completed upper secondary education or higher education and a further 26% hold Standard Grade level 1-3 or other equivalent qualifications (National Statistics UK, 2007b). The experience of school begins early in Scotland, for almost all four year-olds and most three year-olds attend nursery classes. Schooling is compulsory from age 5 to age 16. Primary education is a seven-year programme (P1 to P7) which is offered in local comprehensive schools, built and staffed by Scotland's 32 local councils. Secondary education is a six-year programme (S1 to S6), the first four years of which enrol children aged on average between 12 and 15 (SG, 2007a), while the second two years are post-compulsory. About two-thirds of a cohort of young people stay on for a further year (S5) and 41% continue for an additional year (S6). Secondary schools are also comprehensive establishments under the control of the local authorities.

There are national curriculum guidelines covering school programmes for children aged 5-14. In the final two years of compulsory school (S3/S4), students prepare for examinations, usually in subjects known as Standard Grades, though additional options are available through other national qualifications. The examinations for Standard Grades are set at different levels of difficulty (Foundation, General and Credit), and are prepared in some subjects through ability "setting" (*e.g.*, in mathematics). The approach of differentiated levels in examinations was introduced in the 1980s to support increases in participation to age 16.

Since that time, many more young people have continued at school, and their participation has again been assisted by offering national courses at graduated levels of difficulty. These courses are modular. They comprise units which can be taken separately or as sequences ("courses"). In Scotland, as in the rest of the United Kingdom, there is no statutory concept of an overarching credential which involves defined minimum standards in the number and nature of studies undertaken (graduation requirements). There is, nevertheless, an expectation about this, with universities generally requiring a minimum of exam passes in addition to any specific course requirements. The curriculum of schools is structured in a vertical sense (hierarchy of difficulty). It is mainly academic in nature, with vocational studies mainly delivered through links with Further Education colleges.

At the end of compulsory school, many young Scots enter these colleges. Here they undertake vocational, general and also academic subjects, including at an advanced level. Most college provision, including higher education, is vocational in nature, but it includes some general and academic subjects. Across their range of provision, colleges are major suppliers of higher education in addition to non-advanced courses and training. A declining proportion of young people leaving school also begin a craft apprenticeship. Students who complete a further year of school (S5) also transfer to further education or apprenticeship as well as going on to university (or attempting further exams in S6).

Young people in Scotland enter higher education through different paths—directly from school to university, delayed transition through a "gap year", and enrolment in advanced courses in colleges. Higher education participation for the age-cohort is about 47%, while direct transition from school to higher education is around 30%.

Broadly speaking, Scotland can be described as having a comprehensive system of compulsory schooling with a largely common curriculum to age 14, differentiation by subject difficulty rather than by stream or sector to age 16, and a variable pattern of post-compulsory studies, differentiated again by academic level, but not yielding any common certificate. Segregation by type of school (public, private) is very limited in Scotland, except in Edinburgh.

From an international perspective, formal selection in Scotland is delayed till Standard Grades are attempted (S3/S4), although preceded by "setting" in some subjects, and is then managed informally through the "climbing frame" of national courses offered at different "complexity" levels and through the school-college division of labour between "academic" and "vocational" studies (though this division is not hard and fast).

By European standards, Scotland has a long tradition of education "for the people" (Devine, 1999). It is also one of the first nations to have introduced "modern" subjects into a once mainly classical curriculum. Historically, an enterprising spirit in curriculum coupled with the strength of its universities has made Scotland a net exporter of intellectuals, merchants, and administrators. Throughout the twentieth-century, Scotland turned to its school system to create a more prosperous and equitable nation, and has repeatedly reviewed and reformed its institutional arrangements to achieve this goal.

Economic changes continue to challenge the school system. These relate in part to industries and labour markets (discussed in Chapter 5 of this report). But demographic change is also important. Scotland's population is ageing. This, together with a projected decline in the size of the population to below 5 million by 2036 (COSLA, 2007), will call for greater productivity on the part of younger age-groups, increasing national reliance on immigration, and also greater participation in lifelong learning.

At present, immigration levels are fairly modest. The average net intake over the last five years has been about 10 000 people per year, though for 2004-2005 it was about 20 000. Since enlargement of the European Union in May 2004, there has been a significant increase in migrants from central and eastern Europe. In the longer term, Scotland may experience some of the tensions associated with immigration (including refugee intakes) that have marked other European nations. For example, a high proportion of all asylum seekers live in Glasgow. The largest of these groups are from Iraq, Iran and Somalia (COSLA, 2007). They will be taking their places in classrooms in which there is already a high concentration of children in poverty. So special support may be needed.

Both economic and population changes make it essential that Scottish schools mobilize the energies and abilities of all young people as early as possible, expose them to rewarding intellectual and cultural challenges, and support them beyond what their families may be able to do. For this to happen, it is essential that the institutional arrangements of curriculum, examinations and qualifications work as opportunities and incentives to achievement rather than barriers and bastions of the past.

The cultural renewal of Scotland's people cannot occur through schools alone—in part because there are strong social pressures to use schools as instruments of positional advantage in a highly competitive world. Lifelong learning through further and higher education will become increasingly important as older age-groups seek to adjust to changing environments and demands on them. But the disposition to lifelong learning is itself closely linked with the extent and quality of an individual's experience of school. So the openness, responsiveness and effectiveness of Scotland's schools remain vital.

Strengths of Scottish school education

To the OECD observer, Scottish schools are very energetic and committed enterprises. It is not surprising that the country performs so well on international measures. Only a handful of other nations—Finland, Korea, the Netherlands—can confidently be said to outdo Scotland in PISA mathematical literacy. Fewer than 3 in 100 Scottish 15 year-olds perform very poorly in mathematics—less than half the average for OECD countries. Again only three countries outperform Scotland on reading literacy— Finland, Korea and Canada—and only three can be said confidently to do better in scientific literacy (Finland, Japan, Korea) (Thorpe, 2004. pp. 13, 26, 32).

The consistently high rankings of Scotland on PISA measures are no doubt linked to a range of cultural and historical factors. Scottish society is more culturally homogeneous than many OECD countries. While immigration is increasing, this is far from reaching levels experienced south of the border or in other countries, such as France, Spain, or Ireland. There is less social inequality in Scotland than in the United Kingdom as a whole or in Australia or New Zealand, though more than in Nordic countries (ESRC 2007; UNDP 2007). Scotland has a long tradition of education for all, including for the poorest children, and there has long been a belief in the importance of equity.

But for these cultural factors to give Scotland a comparative advantage requires a set of institutional arrangements which favour the high overall level of achievement and only limited inequality that are the marks of the system. Just what are the strengths of Scottish school education that deliver these two outstanding results?

Approached from one angle, good outcomes for Scottish students rest on a flexible and inclusive curriculum, adaptive teaching, reflective school leadership, and teacher training with a strong practical and contextual emphasis. Approached from a different angle is another set of strengths. These relate to provision and policy. They include primary schools, comprehensive secondary schools, universal pre-school provision, local authority system management, an inspectorate that aims at cultural change and strategic action rather than compliance, and national priorities backed by a real commitment of resources and cross-portfolio policy co-ordination. The diagram in Figure 2.1 sets out these strengths. These are presented from two sides—school culture and programmes, and system provision and policy—and converge on student achievement and progression (or transition).

Figure 2.1 A checklist of Strengths of Scottish School Education

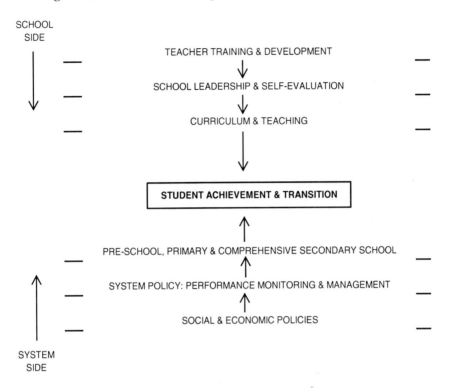

This is a checklist of strengths. Educationalists would argue that every system of schools should have all or most of these strengths. But can Scotland make a convincing claim to having them? High scores on PISA tests do not settle the matter, if only because other measures are available which are not so flattering. While Scotland performs significantly above the international average in the Trends in International Mathematics and Science Study (TIMSS), it is exceeded by many other nations (Mullis *et al.*, 2004).

This OECD review endeavours to highlight strengths, to raise questions and to point to evidence in order to promote discussion. The debate about whether Scotland does well and does enough can gain from being joined by outside observers. For if everything has to be explained to these observers, that can only improve the acuity and the confidence of the Scots themselves.

Universal pre-school provision

Many empirical studies have shown that investment in pre-school delivers lifelong benefits through more rapid cognitive and social growth (Reynolds *et al.*, 2001; Feinstein and Duckworth, 2006). While good quality pre-schooling does not end social inequalities, it reduces them by better preparing children from less well-educated homes to manage the demands of classroom learning. Pre-school moderates the gap in achievement which tends to widen during primary school and which, unchecked, undermines compulsory secondary education in comprehensive schools.

In Scotland, all children aged 3-4 have access to free pre-school education. Accessibility and community are important themes in quality pre-school education. While many children are enrolled in private and voluntary centres (including some that receive local authority grants), the majority attend sessions in primary or nursery schools. The Scottish Government's Pre-School and Childcare Statistics 2007 indicate that in January 2007, some 95.3% of three year-olds and 99.2% of four year-olds were registered for pre-school education with local authorities (SG, 2007b).

With almost all children in the 3-4 age-band attending nursery classes, the challenge of the achievement gap that widens during primary school and which underlies the tensions in comprehensive secondary education is being tackled early. But to ensure that the goals of children's well-being and learning are met amongst all groups, especially in disadvantaged settings, will require higher proportions of qualified and specially trained staff. As Her Majesty's inspectors observe, "While the level of qualifications is increasing overall, around a quarter of staff have no formal childcare qualifications. Many children do not have regular contact with a qualified teacher in learning contexts" (HMIe, 2006i, p. 92).

Primary Schools

When the children of a nation are educated to a high standard, their schools become a natural object of scrutiny. This may be to share lessons about what works well or to ensure that the things that do work well are always kept in view. The greatest strength of Scottish schooling is its primary schools. They educate all children in common—including most of those with special needs—and are thus exposed to the full range of the population. Yet on international measures, such as reading achievement in PIRLS (Progress in International Reading Literacy Study), they perform well above the international average (Mullis *et al.*, 2003). On national measures, such as reading and mathematics levels, high proportions of children are one or two years ahead (as will be seen in Chapter 4). While there are significant gaps in achievement, these have been reduced in recent years, as reflected in findings from the former National Survey of 5-14 Achievement Levels. Perhaps most revealing have been the falls in under-achievement amongst children living in poverty. In 1998/99, every third such child in P5 (nine years old) failed to achieve Level B in writing. But this had been reduced to fewer than 1 in 5 by 2003/04 (The Poverty Site, 2007). Under-achievement had also been reduced in reading and in mathematics, though from less severe levels.

Without this strong platform, Scotland would not be able to operate an effective comprehensive secondary school system or achieve rates of participation in higher education which are comparatively high internationally. However, building a platform which is equally solid for all children is a major continuing challenge. That primary schools are responding so well to this challenge—as indicated by improvement measures—would justify significant increased investment in them, though targeted (as we shall argue in Chapter 7) to where the challenge is most acute.

Comprehensive schooling

Comprehensive secondary schooling is another major strength of Scottish education. We shall review the international evidence in some detail in Chapter 3. However, issues of consistency of quality and greater equity are more pronounced in secondary than in primary schools. It is thus important to reflect on what is valuable in comprehensive schooling as a model of provision—on why and in what ways, it is a major asset, even if, in Scotland, its potential is not being fully realized. Many of the recommendations we make (Chapter 7) relate to secondary schools. For this is where the scope for improvement **on the part of mainly good schools** is greater and the tasks of formulating and operating good policy are more complex.

Many other nations use schools, particularly secondary schools, to divide children from each other. The gains that go to individual families from this practice by no means ensure that a nation as a whole gains (OECD, 2001; OECD, 2005a; Hanushek and Woessmann, 2005; Willms, 2006). This is because a high general standard hinges on exposing all children to challenge, but in shared settings where the presence of strong learners is a source of support and encouragement to weaker learners. To split the cohort and disperse students over many competing sites is to deny them access to each other—access to role models, to "pilot" students (as the French call them), to the stimulus of difference, to the bonds of growing together. In the end, it is to substitute hierarchy for community.

Comprehensive schooling in Scotland has contained levels of social inequality, while supporting higher overall levels of attainment. Studies by Croxford (2000), Croxford and Raffe (2005), and Jenkins, Mickelwright and Schnepf (2006) have shown that Scotland's attachment to a more socially integrated and community-based system of schools has paid dividends. Selective systems elsewhere in Europe have delivered "choice" for some families, but at the price of greater inequality and lower standards (Jesson, 2001; Johnson, 2003).

Nor has Scotland embraced private schooling to any large extent. For only about 3% of primary-aged and just over 5% of secondary-aged pupils are educated in private fee-charging establishments (SE, 2007d). The proportion is very much higher in Edinburgh, where around 20% of S1 and over 33% of S6 pupils are enrolled in the independent sector. But this reflects a concentration of wealth and life-style preferences based on this. Most Scottish parents see school as a community resource. A minority of parents exercise options for non-local enrolment within the publicly-funded system (about 22% in both primary and secondary).

Denominational schools are part of the public system and operate along comprehensive lines. Unlike in other countries, such as Spain and France, where denominational schools are also fully funded by public authorities, faith schools in Scotland have not drawn criticism for being socially or academically selective and for leaving more difficult tasks to local public schools. Indeed the history of Catholic schools in Scotland has been marked by quite a different emphasis.

One test of the cohesion of comprehensive systems relates to the degree of tension experienced during the critical transition years between the end of primary school and the beginning of post-compulsory school. It is during the compulsory years of secondary education that stresses of both a pedagogical and a social nature tend to be most intense. In European countries where the transition to comprehensive schooling has experienced the greatest historical resistance—examples include England and France (despite the latter's commitment to the *collège unique*)—these stresses have been acute and there has been no satisfactory resolution, either through rigid top-down administration or through quasi-market policies. Scotland, by contrast with these countries, displays much less tension in compulsory secondary education. This suggests that comprehensive schooling enjoys wide cultural acceptance and support.

Comprehensive schooling is a strength because it enables communities to pool economic and cultural resources in schools that are widely accessible. This does not mean that all children have access to the same pool of resources, *e.g.*, the same cultural mix of pupils. For residential segregation divides communities and produces differentially high or low concentrations of cultural as well as economic resources. However, as we shall see, where comprehensive schooling is backed by an appropriate system of public administration, as in Scotland, the effects of residential segregation can be tackled, which is not necessarily the case with market-based (Lamb, 2007).

The question that needs to be raised is whether the potential of comprehensive schooling is fully exploited in Scotland. In theory, the pooling of financial resources in schools under local authority control should mean a wider range of programs and greater flexibility in how teachers are employed—two key elements in improving quality of student learning for all groups. The pooling of cultural resources, on the other hand, should favour a school culture of high expectations and aspirations, strong positive peer effects on learning, and improvements in teacher morale and commitment (Willms, 2006). Moreover, if local authorities successfully tackle resource imbalances between schools and if school leaders, for their part, effectively mobilize resources within their schools, student learning differences should be minimized, first between schools and secondly within schools.

Whether this potential is fully realized by the comprehensive system in Scotland is a matter of debate, to which this report under different headings seeks to contribute.

Local education authorities

The strong performance of many Scottish schools points to another major strength of Scottish education: the system of local education authorities through which these are provided. The importance of local authorities should be seen in the context, not only of what they achieve in education—as attested in the inspectorate's recent assessment of their effectiveness (HMIe, 2006e)—but the operation of alternative models of school system management.

In recent decades, governments have been under pressure to tackle school improvement through devolution of school management and also through marketisation policies. Scotland, by contrast with some other systems (including England), has relied more on local government to deliver quality schooling, and has done so successfully. Market policies have made little headway. The emphasis on public administration through local authorities, backed up by independent inspection of both schools and local councils, recognizes the unequal potential of market policies to deliver quality to all sections of a community. On the other hand, the potential of local administrations to ensure high quality outcomes for all children may not be fully realized where schools lack a significant degree of management autonomy, for example, in staffing matters.

Views about the real level of school management autonomy in Scotland differ, depending on the perspective of the observer. Local authorities stress the powers that they devolve to schools, while headteacher organisations complain of the lack of flexibility that schools experience. The scale of the challenges facing some urban communities in Scotland does point to the need for strong local administrations, capable of harnessing, co-ordinating and targeting resources effectively. But this does not rule out greater management autonomy for schools, particularly in areas such as staffing and curriculum. Such an approach—of devolved management within a framework of local government— recognizes the very unequal social environments in which children attend schools and the need to maximise the flexibility of schools, while at the same time ensuring a balanced and effective allocation of resources and services across schools. Over half the population of Glasgow lives in the most deprived 15% of local areas in Scotland (HMIe, 2006e, p. 12-13). As HMI observe, at least one-quarter of Dundee City, Inverclyde, North Lanarkshire and West Dunbartonshire are in the 15% most deprived areas nationally, and even some advantaged areas have substantial pockets of disadvantage.

Placing schools under local authority control potentially increases community inputs to decision-making and greater communication about needs and initiatives. It also enables a range of human services to be "joined up" through a client-centred approach, based on local knowledge of family circumstances and priorities. Local authorities are repositories of professional knowledge and experience which are pooled and distributed to schools through centrally-provided services and ongoing consultation and quality assurance. Innovations and good practice developed at one site in a school system can be communicated to other sites, thanks to the mediating role of professional officers and through continuing professional development organized by the local authority. Schools are not left to fend for themselves, but are both "challenged and supported". However, their capacity to respond to challenges hinges on how much control they effectively exercise over the two key resources they possess—their teachers and the curriculum.

While community-based public administration has much to recommend it, making it work well across 32 local authorities of very divergent character is a major challenge. Those with the highest densities of deprivation are committed to raising aspirations and improving student engagement; they measure their impact and are able to point to the interventions which work. They are innovative, for example, in strategies to improve attendance and in inclusive practices for children with special needs (HMIe, 2006e, p. 12-13). Tellingly, the best local authorities target support to curriculum. For it is through curriculum that demands and expectations are raised on students, while creating accessible and meaningful opportunities for success. Pre-school provision has been assessed as a strength in almost all education authorities (HMIe, 2006e, p. 12-13). There is clear evidence of overall improvements in student learning, particularly in the early primary years. However, it is proving difficult to build on these gains in upper primary and secondary school, and HMI consider that the performance of local authorities continues to vary too much (HMIe, 2006e, p. 27).

The uneven performance of local government in the education field raises questions about the consistency of existing institutional arrangements. For example, local authorities build schools, pay teachers, and organize professional development. However, they appear to have little influence over the national curriculum. This has not stopped some local authorities, such as North Lanarkshire, from undertaking reforms of a nationally significant character. But why has this not occurred more widely when the absence of a nationally prescribed curriculum should allow, if not encourage on-the-ground reform? Lack of influence over curriculum reduces the capacity of local government to influence pathways to further education and work, and this is again reduced by the institutional automony of the colleges. When there is considerable and persistent regional variation in attainment and transition, the consistency of arrangements governing curriculum and programme provision is inevitably called into question. Scotland has not chosen a market model of autonomous schools to drive improvement, but on the other hand the devolution of power to local government appears to be limited in a number of key areas, and this in turn may be discouraging schools from making the changes that improvement requires.

Leadership of schools

Scottish schools face a future of rising expectations and a past of inherited inequalities. The kind of citizen that schools are expected to form in the future must be seen against the kind of society within which schools must work. Society sets up high expectations about the well-educated man or woman of the future—for example, through a *Curriculum for Excellence*—while creating environments of very unequal distance from which to pursue the ideal. It is left to schools to resolve the conflict between expectations and reality, between the future and the past. The deeper the conflict, the greater the demand on those qualities of human enterprise, ingenuity, vision and courage that we call leadership.

Headteachers of Scotland's primary schools are assessed in most cases as "very good" (39%) or "good" (44%). The criteria for these positive assessments include demonstrable commitment to quality of learning and teaching, pupil well-being, rapport with staff, and relationships with their communities and with outside agencies (HMIe, 2006e, p. 32). Integrating the efforts of schools through teamwork, a shared focus on student learning, a sharing of professional experience, and monitoring of progress helps build a culture of self-evaluation and continuous improvement. It is significant that some Scottish primary schools solicit the views of pupils on quality of learning and teaching. This creates a vital feedback loop. It reveals a willingness to test efforts and to risk a visibility that schools in other countries are frequently loath to do.

On the other hand, there are weaknesses in the leadership of a minority of primary schools. These include lack of vision and strategic focus on teaching and learning, poor rapport with staff and with the external world, and failure to develop or apply measures of self-evaluation. Almost 1 in 5 Scottish primary schools are assessed as merely "fair" or even "unsatisfactory" under these headings (HMIe, 2006, p. 32).

Broadly similar observations regarding quality of leadership apply to Scottish secondary schools. Over 80% are assessed as good or very good, but with a significant minority failing in areas such as school climate or ethos, lack of integration in terms of roles and teamwork, and inadequate progress in student learning. Secondary schools, through their subject departments and more complex management structures, face some distinctive leadership challenges. But the most important issue is the gap in pupil attainment, especially in lower secondary classes, notwithstanding improvements in recent years.

As many as 40% of secondary schools are assessed as only "fair" (or "unsatisfactory") on overall quality of attainment of pupils in S1/S2 (HMIe, 2006e, p. 36). While assessments based on inspection are better at S3/S4, every third school is still judged as only fair or unsatisfactory. This finding underlines the importance of the recruitment and training of headteachers. An impressive feature of Scottish education is the programme through which future leaders achieve the Standard for Headship. The Scottish Qualification for Headship (SQH) is a demanding course which was introduced in 1998. An innovative programme, it combines university study with two practical projects, based in school. The projects are keyed to needs in the candidate's school, and the candidate is supported by the headteacher or other senior member of staff. Normally the course requires part-time study over four years, but there is an accelerated version for candidates already exercising senior management roles in schools. The SQH is highly rated by graduates, their headteachers, and the directors of education in the local authorities (SE, 2003).

It is a major initiative which involves problem-based learning in the workplace, mentorship, alignment with professional development needs in school, structured training in core management functions (Learning and Teaching; Policy, Planning, and Finance; Accountability, etc.), and broad flow-on benefits in the form of staff cohesion and commitment. Of international significance, the SQH will assist Scottish schools to break the nexus between social environment and student achievement and to respond effectively to the heightened expectations on student learning in the twenty-first century. However, given retirement levels in the next five years, are sufficient numbers of future headteachers undertaking the programme?

Teachers

Scotland has undertaken a major investment in its teaching force. Appropriately, there has been a focus on working arrangements in schools. A 35-hour working week was introduced in 2001 as part of the national Teachers' Agreement. Maximum class contact time for primary teachers was reduced to 23.5 hours in 2004-2005 (aligning with secondary teachers), with a further reduction to 22.5 hours from the 1st. of August, 2006. A new career structure was introduced in 2002, and recruitment of an extra 3 500 support staff was scheduled for completion in 2004.

These changes were seen as important in helping to create effective learning environments in schools, offering career incentives for professional development, and freeing teachers to focus their efforts on student learning. Viewed in an international perspective, the suite of changes introduced by the Teachers' Agreement represents an important case-study in addressing key issues of attracting and retaining good teachers in schools. Amongst these issues are creating productive operating conditions, giving teachers the flexibility to exercise their professional skills, supporting teachers through ancillary staff, and implementing attractive programmes of professional development (OECD, 2005b).

Under the Agreement, Scottish teachers have an obligation to undertake continuing professional development (CPD). From August 2003, a compulsory 35 hours of CPD per year was introduced. Importantly, this programme was to be negotiated within schools between teachers and their supervisors, "taking into account ... school, local and national priorities" (HMIe, 2007, p. 19). It was also to be backed by an annual review process. Implemented by local authorities, the review process has contributed to a greater commitment on the part of teachers to self-evaluation and more interest in training opportunities.

Teachers received a pay increase of 23.5% between 2001 and 2003 and part of a further increase of 10.4% between 2004 and 2007 (HMIe, 2007, p. 23). Starting salaries for teachers were also brought into line with the average salary of graduates. The inspectorate's report on implementation of the Teachers' Agreement notes that this was a key factor in improving recruitment, with applicants for post-graduate training rising by 26% in primary and 40% in secondary over the period 2002-2005.

Scotland's approach to renewing the teaching force and focussing teaching on inclusive and effective learning has thus involved a combination of improving operating conditions in schools, on the one hand, and boosting financial and career incentives, on the other. In the long term, it is attention to the quality of the school as a well-supported laboratory of teaching practice that will do most to ensure that even the most challenging settings have a strong and effective workforce.

In many countries, schools rely on universities for the initial training of teachers, and there are international concerns about the quality and effectiveness of pre-service programmes. In Scotland, the professional placement period for trainee teachers is quite high—30 weeks over the four years of an undergraduate program and three periods of five weeks in post-graduate programmes. For secondary teachers, though, there is a perception in some schools that training remains too subject-centred and too little focussed on the challenges of diversity and inclusiveness.

Of particular note in the professional training of teachers are the provisions of the Teachers' Agreement relating to probationers. The Agreement guarantees that all probationers will have a one-year training contract in a single school, with a maximum class commitment of 0.7 FTE (HMIe, 2007, p. 25). During the OECD visit to Scotland, the Scottish approach to induction was highly praised by recent probationers. Trained induction managers, mentoring, and class-free time for reflection and professional observation were seen as helping create a very supportive environment. Induction is a crucial link in the itinerary of new teachers who, too frequently in many countries in the past, were left to fend for themselves, often in more "hard to staff" schools which relied ineffectually on a continuing supply of new recruits to manage high turnover. However, concerns have been expressed regarding the extent to which probationers obtain teaching posts at the end of their induction year.

Schools visited by the OECD team reported that new teachers were enthusiastic and highly committed. A sustained practicum, followed by carefully managed and supported induction, no doubt contribute greatly to the confidence and the preparedness of new teachers, while major revisions to the salary scale are now attracting young people to the profession who could well choose other career paths.

Curriculum

Breadth of curriculum is a major strength of primary education in Scotland (HMIe, 2006i, p. 28). It is a feature which might be taken for granted, though in those countries which place a heavy emphasis on testing in a few core areas, it cannot be assumed (McMurrer, 2007). The importance of breadth lies partly in the developmental needs of children. They grow cognitively and socially at different rates, and the stimulus of a wide range of activities and experiences is needed for all to grow well and fully. But, equally, the intrinsic value of activities, such as music, art, and drama, argues in favour of breadth. HMIe observe that in "almost all primary schools, the curriculum is well-structured. Schools are using the national 5-14 curriculum guidelines to offer breadth and consistency of experience for all" (HMIe, 2006i, p. 28).

There is no statutory curriculum in Scotland. While respecting the guidelines, schools can use up to 20% of teaching time to offer activities of particular local relevance. This gives scope for addressing issues of low achievement, poor motivation, and behavioural problems. Not all schools exploit the flexibility that the 20% provision represents, and thus lose valuable opportunities. Since *A Curriculum for Excellence* will extend more freedom to schools, this is likely to be a continuing concern. Curriculum reform has to come from schools themselves rather than waiting for central directions.

In secondary schools, Scottish pupils also have access to a broad curriculum (HMIe, 2006i, p. 41). The question is whether "breadth" is translated into opportunities for the whole age-group to move forward or whether breadth is interpreted more as a compliance issue with regard to timetabled classes. The early years of secondary school show a weakening in student learning as more complex material is introduced. If curriculum is operated as a rigid structure, the time and the resources needed to tackle this problem will not be available. The time will be for subjects, not students.

Significantly, an increasing number of schools are introducing vocational options in S3/S4 and operating the curriculum as a source of flexibility and adaptability. Skills for Work courses and Enterprise activities figure prominently (HMIe, 2006m, p. 11). Schools appear to be making greater use of college links to broaden the curriculum that is effectively available to students, especially weaker learners. Whether it is a strength that such students regain motivation mainly for the studies they do at college (HMIe, 2006i, p. 41), does raise a question about the impact on the curriculum and culture of the school in relying on the college to manage student needs in this way. As we shall discuss later in this report, to harness the full potential of vocational studies requires a broad view, both of the role of these studies themselves and of the cognitive, social and economic needs of young people. The current Scottish approach appears to be rather narrowly focussed on employability, and indeed even the view of employability itself may be too limited.

Scotland has taken a distinctive approach to the organisation of the curriculum in the last two years of compulsory school. In their final year (S4)—and sometimes in S3—pupils present for examinations which are set at different levels: Foundation, General, and Credit. This gives all pupils access to national certification at the end of compulsory schooling. The Standard Grade reforms were implemented in the early 1980s, following the Munn and Dunning reviews. They created space for a broader range of children to continue their schooling beyond age 14 and to have their achievements recognized.

The final years of compulsory school are a critical phase for many children. This is because the demands of the curriculum become more intense and specialized, and teaching often more conservative and subject-centred, while family and school support structures tend to weaken. In some countries, *e.g.*, Spain, this leads to high rates of failure and also to high, if declining reliance on grade-repeating in a bid to restore chances. While, in that country, there may be legal scope to vary the curriculum and thus to moderate cognitive demands on pupils, there is no framework within the curriculum itself which protects weaker pupils from the severity of academic culture. Thus, even in the absence of national examinations, every fourth child in Spain fails compulsory secondary education (Teese *et al.*, 2006).

Scotland draws all children into the curriculum, but recognizes that they will learn at different rates and more or less unevenly. From a developmental perspective, to examine pupils at age 16 is arbitrary, but it is both arbitrary and potentially damaging to purport to offer a definitive measure of their capacities at that age, even in domains of more academic learning. Moderating the levels at which pupils are assessed is a way of solving a major problem: how to give children from all family backgrounds access to the intellectual and cultural demands of the curriculum—which includes being able to study subjects **and** be assessed at a suitable level—while certifying differences between them in how they fulfill these demands.

Standard Grades are not an unproblematic solution to this problem. They have raised attainment levels and provide a reward and a testimony to what children have achieved who, in some other countries, are failed and who describe themselves as "zero" (Dubet, 2006, p. 42-43). But individual access to different levels of assessment may be accompanied by unequal access to the curriculum through subject setting. Moreover, it may be questioned whether the basic strategy of lowering the examinations platform (Gamoran, 1996) is sufficient incentive to engage learners **in the absence of innovations in curriculum content and emphasis.**

It is this latter concern which highlights the potential of the Skills for Work courses that began to be implemented in Scottish schools from 2005. Intended for S3 pupils and above, these courses aim to develop "practical vocational skills and to improve...employment prospects by developing a range of employability skills" (LTS, undated). Skills for Work courses provide core general skills as well as practical skills in vocational areas (SE, 2005a, Annex C). But they may be seen as at somewhat of a tangent to mainstream studies, and their potential to promote a different approach to learning more widely may be missed by relying on colleges to deliver them.

A second major initiative in diversifying the curriculum—including in primary schools—is Enterprise Education. Under the Determined to Succeed: Enterprise in Education programme, all students over the age of 14 have an entitlement to work-based vocational learning. To implement this, partnership agreements have been established between schools and local businesses and other organisations. A target of 2 000 such agreements was set for the whole of Scotland by 2006 (a minimum of five agreements per school cluster) (SE, 2003d, p. 15). By 2007, over 7 000 agreements had been signed.

Again, this approach to curriculum diversity should be seen in an international perspective. Some countries choose to stream or track, including from age 14, and segregate children. This has been shown to increase social inequalities. Moreover, withdrawing a large proportion of children from general programmes in schools is not necessarily the best strategy for satisfying national skill needs over the long term. For it is higher-order cognitive, organisational and communication skills that service economies demand.

Skills for Work and Enterprise in Education programmes open up the space of the curriculum rather than simply lowering the bar to ensure limited access to a largely academic space. These initiatives should be seen in a broader framework of questions about how students learn (not only whether they become more employable), about the incentives offered to them to become more committed learners (including in academic programmes), and about transforming approaches to teaching and learning across the curriculum (including the use of different physical settings for learning, such as the workplace and community projects).

In Scotland, progression to upper secondary education was impeded until the mid-1990s by a lack of articulation between Standard Grades and the mainly academic programmes of Highers, leading to university. Students did have access to vocational modules, but these lacked status and coherence as study options (Raffe, Howieson and Tinklin, 2007). The Higher Still reforms that were carried through in the 1990s extended to post-compulsory school the structural solution represented by Standard Grades. But this was applied more widely to curriculum, not only to assessment. Subjects could be studied at different levels—Intermediate 1, Intermediate 2, Highers, and Advanced Highers.

The National Qualifications, introduced in the 1990s, differentiated levels of curriculum for the benefit of the whole range of students. As well as addressing the needs of average and high achievers, they expanded the space of the curriculum to accommodate less academically successful students. As National Qualifications are modular, they offer considerable flexibility, being combined in different ways and taken as units or courses, depending on interest and availability. Both the graduated cognitive level of subjects and their modular construction offer important advantages over curriculum systems of a more traditional kind, where students must take full courses (year-long subjects) and where graduation may require structured combinations and threshold requirements, all of which can become barriers to participation and achievement.

As with Standard Grades, however, questions remain about whether the solution of structured levels and modular flexibility ranges widely enough over the fields of academic and applied learning, and whether, at the point of delivery, there is broad and effective choice. The curriculum is an engine of achievement. Its purpose is to challenge and extend individuals. So it must be designed and delivered in such a way as to make real and accessible demands on all students. The solution to low achievement is not to relax demands and lower expectations, but to exert pressure and secure engagement through more pedagogically effective and incentive-based curricula.

Qualifications

It is partly because secondary education in Scotland is a flexible structure and partly because the delivery of the curriculum is shared between schools and colleges that a framework has been developed which maps formal (and eventually also non-formal) learning to differentiated levels of qualification, including beyond school. The Scottish Credit and Qualifications Framework (SCQF) classifies study and training options at different levels of difficulty ("complexity"), and aims to enable them to be taken in different combinations (with accumulating credit) and to be recognized across different institutional settings. Any accredited unit or course of study occupies the same place in this framework, regardless of the status or sector of the provider delivering it. Thus, a student can move seamlessly across the SCQF within the same study area, but at different levels of difficulty, and also across areas, with progression governed by the effective pace of learning of the individual.

The classification of qualifications by complexity level and credit points potentially gives the learner freedom from two institutional constraints—the sector or setting where learning occurs (geography of the education system) and the point in time when learning occurred (and thus the history of qualifications). For example, a student can accumulate credits from Standard Grades taken at school and National Courses or units undertaken at college. The providers are different ("geography") and the qualifications have different origins ("history"). But the SCQF harmonises the levels and ignores the setting. Since bodies of knowledge are contained in a variety of study units, developed under different circumstances—*e.g.*, the Standard Grade reforms or the National Qualifications—and since, moreover, they may be delivered in different sectors, the SCQF frees access to them and bypasses institutions in favour of individuals.

Implemented in December 2001, the SCQF has made Scotland a leader in European efforts to harmonise qualifications, both in higher education and in VET (Gallacher *et al.*, 2005.) The role of the SCQF for school students—including their access to courses in colleges—is perhaps more developed than in tertiary education, where credit transfer issues continue to be more formal than real. However, the role for school students points to an issue which the SCQF helps manage, but does not resolve. The curriculum in secondary education is in effect split across institutional sectors (as in the academic and vocational divide, between schools and colleges, and between educational and employment settings), and to the extent that it is based in schools, it is split across two different historical frameworks (Standard Grades and National Qualifications). The "national vocabulary" of the SCQF enables individuals to reach across these divides, but it does not harmonise or maximize provision as such. The fact that SVQs are not available to school students highlights the point that the SCQF does not fully bridge the worlds of school and work.

Pathways and transition support

To lift and support the educational effort of young people, Scotland has taken a number of major steps: (a) reformed the upper secondary curriculum, diversifying options and enlarging choice; (b) expanded vocational education for S3/S4 students through Skills for Work programmes, Enterprise initiatives, and national courses other than Standard Grades; and (c) extended or developed "lateral" links between schools and enterprises, and between schools and colleges, to vary the setting and the emphasis in student learning.

Attainment levels have risen, creating a stronger platform for young people to extend their efforts and invest in post-compulsory education or training. Improvements have also been recorded in student satisfaction with school. There have been significant, measured rises in the extent to which young people feel that school has given them "confidence to make decisions" and "taught me things useful in a job". Conversely, there has been a fall in the extent to which young people feel that "school has done little to prepare me for life when I leave school" (Croxford, 2003). These improvements have been greater in Scotland than in England. Moreover, they hold, after adjusting for gains in attainment.

While greater student confidence and satisfaction with school may be due to a range of social factors, there are grounds for thinking that reformed institutional arrangements have had a significant impact, both directly and indirectly. For improved structures of opportunity have been put in place— giving young people greater scope to use school and to succeed—and student attainment has risen.

From the academic year 2007/08, Careers Scotland will ensure that every young person who plans to leave school will be offered a face-to-face consultation with a Careers Scotland Adviser. Careers Scotland will also provide increased early intervention and one-to-one support and advice to young people who require additional targeted support. Careers Scotland monitors student transition and provides transition feedback to schools and local authorities. Young people thus have a clearer view of the landscape of education, training and employment opportunities available on leaving school, and they receive individual support in planning the directions that are open to them and that interest them.

An expanded structure of opportunities, student support services, rising levels of attainment, and greater student satisfaction and confidence have all contributed to a trend in which more and more young people invest in post-school education and training (even though there has been no recent change in the proportions continuing in school). Thus, between 1993 and 2006, the number of school leavers entering full-time higher education rose from 25% of a cohort to 30% (Careers Scotland, 2007u). There were also increases in numbers undertaking non-advanced courses in colleges. While this did not completely offset the long-term decline in young people undertaking employment-based training (including apprenticeships), it represents a very significant adjustment. For schools and colleges have responded well to the challenge posed by declining training opportunities and have enabled large numbers of young people to manage the loss of apprenticeships through greater use of college.

Not all young people have benefitted from improvements in school programs, student support services, and access to colleges. It is estimated that some 36 000 young people aged 16-19 years are not in education, training or employment (NEET) (SE, 2007d, p. 42). While many do move into employment or education (44%), the majority of this diverse group tend to continue in unemployment or remain inactive. The roots of poor transition are complex, and the issues facing individuals vary considerably. National policy relies on vigorous strategies implemented by local authorities to tackle this issue, particularly in those regions of Scotland where poor transition is especially high. Since these regions are generally also ones of high deprivation, there is a question as to whether enduring and significant improvement can be achieved without greater policy co-ordination across portfolios at a national level.

A second issue is whether the definition of NEET adequately captures the extent of economic and social precariousness experienced by young people in Scotland. In other words, the problem may be bigger than current estimates indicate, thus adding to pressures on how policies are framed, implemented and co-ordinated. This is further discussed in Chapter 5 of this report.

Performance monitoring and improvement support

Scotland has established a range of processes for monitoring the performance of its school system. These include the Scottish Survey of Achievement (SSA) (replacing the former National Survey), the Scottish School Leavers Survey (SSLS), destinations monitoring by Careers Scotland, reporting on National Qualifications, and a national statistics service which produces a wealth of readily accessible information. In addition, each local authority monitors patterns and trends in student attainment and transition, and some local authorities supply their schools with benchmarked data.

Recent work on developing a framework for measuring school performance will assist schools and local authorities to make comparisons, adjusted for multiple contextual and intake factors (Maxwell, 2007). The purpose of such comparisons is to help schools evaluate their efforts, after controlling as much as possible for the influence of environments (through a "like schools" methodology). The purpose is not to establish league tables which provide a narrow and misleading view of performance, no tools to interpret rankings, no information on stability of rankings, and no diagnostic or planning utility to aid improvement.

While all these sources of information help schools reflect on their work, they are passive and depend on the culture of leadership in schools as to how well they are used, if at all. By contrast, regular inspections by HMIe are an interactive process. They introduce a defined frame of reference which is external to the school (*How good is our school?*). But inspections also involve informed exchanges between schools and experienced observers (including seconded headteachers). By creating an interactive situation of ongoing dialogue, inspection promotes a culture of self-reflection and evaluation. Potentially this extends to parents, all of whom receive copies of inspection reports, an important Scottish initiative which stands in marked contrast to the publication of league tables elsewhere.

Strategies of school improvement necessarily occur within the circumscribed space of a school and its catchment area, the contours of which they cannot alter. But continuous improvement is important at every point in the space of a school system, particularly in the most "exposed" or vulnerable sites, and even if gains are modest. Inspection provides a spur to improvement, while harnessing the experience of the school system as a whole and channelling it to the sites that stand most in need of it.

The scope of inspection has been extended to include the work of local authorities. This introduces the dynamic of informed exchange to a higher level of educational organisation, and one that is crucial to the equitable performance of Scottish schools.

System policies and strategic management

Scotland enters the twenty-first century burdened with the inequalities and institutional rigidities of the past and facing a future which will entrench these without clear-sighted and vigorous leadership. While incomes are rising, many Scots continue to live in poverty. They are the children of displaced and dispirited workers, and they themselves and their children, too, may be unemployed. Engulfing them are the economic storms of globalization which have already destroyed shipping and the incipient electronics industry of Inverclyde, to name only the more obvious casualties. It is a sad irony, as Scottish headteachers serving the poorest communities point out, that adversity can weaken resolve instead of strengthening it. But have some parents lost faith in education simply because they cannot see where it has ever led them and their own? Or is it because education itself has become a much more powerful institution on which the most well-educated families rely a great deal more than in the past and which today offers too few points of purchase to the poor?

The national priorities set out by the Scottish Government in *Ambitious, Excellent Schools* (2004) recognized that the structure of opportunities and rewards which school represents must be made more inclusive, accessible and rich in economic as well as cultural incentives. There is an emphasis on weakening the rigidities of the system, so that schools have more flexibility, teachers more freedom, and students more choice. At the same time, the stakes are being raised. *A Curriculum for Excellence* demands a wider and deeper effort from all schools in forming "successful learners, effective contributors, confident individuals, and responsible citizens" (SE, 2004, Foreword). Delivering on this agenda requires a major investment of resources (co-ordinated across portfolios) as well as fundamental change in how schools work.

On the first of these challenges, the investment of resources in Scottish school education has been impressive—a major building programme, with 300 new or substantially refurbished schools by 2009, an additional 3 000 teachers against a falling roll of some 50 000 pupils, smaller class sizes, large salary increases, and a very deliberate tackling of quality in human resources through teacher training, induction and headship programmes.

Besides these general measures, there has been a targeting of additional resources to the needs of particular groups, such as "at risk" young people, and a policy of joining up human services to address the multi-sided nature of deprivation. Whether measures to overcome deprivation are sufficiently broadly-based, adequate, properly targeted and co-ordinated across government is an issue. However, there has been a determination to tackle systemic disadvantage, firstly through the Social Justice Strategy (1999-2004), and then through Closing the Opportunity Gap (SE, 2007d, p. 49-50).

Nesting educational objectives within a whole-of-government approach recognizes that the impact of schools is continually blunted by environments of poor housing, low income, high unemployment, and health problems which cross generations. Closing the Gap aims at sustained employment for the vulnerable and disadvantaged, greater financial security for low-income families, the regeneration of neighbourhoods in decay, improved health care, and access to high-quality human services. Progress on these social fronts will enable schools to focus on educational goals, and to work more confidently towards targeted reductions in precarious transition (NEET), higher attainment amongst weaker learners, and enhanced student support.

Cultural change in schools—the second major challenge—cannot come without real national commitment to quality of education services. This is borne out by the discouragement and demoralization of teachers in the 1980s as compared with the enthusiasm and engagement which is evident today, especially in schools serving the most depressed communities. The question is whether the institutional arrangements represented by curriculum, assessment, and qualifications provide sufficient opportunities and incentives to give full expression to this will to make a difference.

References

Careers Scotland (2007u), Unpublished tables on school leaver transitions.

COSLA website (2007), "Strategic migration partnership", *http://www.asylumscotland.org.uk/asylumstatistics.php*

Croxford, L. (2000), "Inequality in attainment at age 16: a 'home international' comparison", *CES Briefing*, No. 19, University of Edinburgh: Centre for Educational Sociology, Edinburgh.

Croxford, L. (2003), "Education and youth transition in England, Wales and Scotland since 1984", Paper for the European Network on Transitions in Youth Conference.
http://www.fdewb.unimaas.nl/roa/tiy2003/papers/L.Croxford.pdf

Croxford, L. and D. Raffe (2005), "Secondary school organisation in England, Scotland and Wales since the 1980s", Paper for the seminar on Policy Learning in 14-19 Education, Joint Seminar of education and youth transitions Project and Nuffield review of 14 – 19 Education, 15 March 2005.

Devine, T.M. (1999), *The Scottish Nation 1700 – 2000?*, Allen Lane, London.

Dubet, F. (2006), "Ce que l'école fait aux vaincus" in Chapelle, G. and D. Meuret (eds.), *Améliorer l'école*, PUF, Paris, pp. 37-49.

ESRC (2007), ESRC Society Today – Knowledge Economy,
http://www.esrc.ac.uk/ESRCInfoCentre/facts/UK/index4.aspx?Compone ntId=6978&SourcePageId=18132

Feinstein, F. and K. Duckworth (2006), *Development in the Early Years: its importance for school performance and adult outcomes*, Centre for Research on the Wider Benefits of Learning, London.

Gallacher, J. *et al.* (2005), *Evaluation of the impact of the Scottish Credit and Qualifications Framework (SCQF)*, Scottish Executive, Edinburgh.

Gamoran, A. (1996), "Curriculum standardization and equality of opportunity in Scottish secondary education, 1984-1990", *Sociology of Education*, No. 69, pp. 1-21.

Hanushek, E.A. and L. Woessmann (2005), "Does educational tracking affect performance and inequality?: Differences-in-differences evidence across countries." Discussion Paper No. 1901, Institute for the Study of Labor (IZA), Bonn

HMIe (2006e), *Improving Scottish Education: Effectiveness of Education Authorities*, Her Majesty's Inspectorate of Education, Livingston.

HMIe (2006i), *Improving Scottish Education*, Her Majesty's Inspectorate of Education, Livingston.

HMIe (2006m), *Missing Out: A report on children at risk of missing out on educational opportunities,* Her Majesty's Inspectorate of Education, Livingston.

HMIe (2007), *Teaching Scotland's Children: report on progress in implementing 'A Teaching Profession for the 21st. Century',* Her Majesty's Inspectorate of Education, Livingston.

Jenkins, S.P., Micklewright, J. and S.V. Schnepf (2006), "Social Segregation in Secondary Schools: How does England compare with other countries?" Applications and Policy Working Paper A06/01, University of Southamptom: Southampton Statistical Sciences Research Institute, Southampton.

Jesson, D. (2001), "Selective systems of schooling - blueprint for lower standards?" *www.york.ac.uk/depts/econ/documents/research/21pbrf3.pdf*

Johnson, M. (2003), *Not choice, but champion. A new look at secondary admissions in London*, Institute for Public Policy Research, London.

Lamb, S. (2007), "School Reform and Inequality in Urban Australia: A Case of Residualizing the Poor" in Teese, R., Lamb, S. and M. Duru-Bellat (eds.), *International Studies in Educational Inequality, Theory and Policy: Vol. 3*, Springer, Dordrecht, pp. 1-38.

LTS (Learning and Teaching Scotland website) (undated), "National Qualifications online: Skills for Work", *http://www.ltscotland.org.uk/nq/nqframework/skillsforwork.asp*

Maxwell, B. (2007), "Using data and performance indicators to promote equity and fair comparisons between schools", Presentation to the OECD Equity Conference, Trondheim.

McMurrer, J. (2007), *Choices, Changes, and Challenges. Curriculum and Instruction in the NCLB Era: A report in the series From the Capital to the Classroom; Year 5 of the No Child Left Behind Act,* Center on Education Policy, Washington, D.C.

Mullis, I.V.S. *et al.* (2004), *TIMSS 2003 International Mathematics Report*, Boston College, Chestnut Hill, MA.

Mullis, I.V.S. *et al.* (2003), *PIRLS 2001 International Report: IEA's Study of Reading Literacy Achievement in Primary Schools,* Boston College, Chestnut Hill, MA.

National Statistics UK (2007b), "Population of working age: by highest qualification, Spring 2003", *Regional Trends 38*, Central Statistics Office, London.

OECD (2001), *Knowledge and Skills for Life,* Organisation for Economic Co-operation and Development, Paris.

OECD (2005a), *School Factors related to Quality and Equity*, Organisation for Economic Co-operation and Development, Paris.

OECD (2005b), *Attracting, Developing and Retaining Effective Teachers – Final Report: Teachers Matter,* Organisation for Economic Co-operation and Development, Paris.

Raffe, D., Howieson, C., and T. Tinklin, (2007), "The impact of a unified curriculum and qualifications system: the Higher Still reform of post-16 education in Scotland", *British Educational Research Journal*, Vol. 33 (in press).

Reynolds, A.J. *et al.* (2001), "Long-term effects of an early childhood intervention on educational achievement and juvenile arrest", *Journal of the American Medical Association*, Vol. 285, pp. 2339-2346.

SED (Scottish Education Department) (1977), *Assessment for All: Report of the Committee to review assessment in the third and fourth years of secondary education in Scotland (The Dunning report)*, Scottish Education Department, HMSO, Edinburgh.

SED (Scottish Education Department) (1977a), *The Structure of the Curriculum in the Third and Fourth Years of the Scottish Secondary School (The Munn report),* Scottish Education Department, Consultative Committee on Curriculum, Edinburgh.

SEED (Scottish Executive Education Department) (2003), *Insight 8: Scottish Qualification for Headship: key issues from the evaluation,* Scottish Executive, Edinburgh.

SEED (Scottish Executive Education Department) (2003d), *Determined to Succeed: Enterprise in Education: Scottish Executive response,* Scottish Executive, Edinburgh.

SEED (Scottish Executive Education Department) (2004), *Ambitious, Excellent Schools: our agenda for action,* Scottish Executive, Edinburgh.

SEED (Scottish Executive Education Department) (2004c), *A Curriculum for Excellence,* The Curriculum Review Group, Edinburgh.

SEED (Scottish Executive Education Department) (2005a), *A Review of collaboration between schools and further education colleges: consultation analysis report of responses to interim report and outline draft strategy,* Scottish Executive, Edinburgh.

Scottish Executive Education Department (2007), *OECD Review of the Quality and Equity of Education Outcomes in Scotland: Diagnostic Report,* available on the OECD website http://dx.doi.org/10.1787/148012367602 or www.oecd.org/edu/reviews/nationalpolicies.

SG (Scottish Government) (2007a), *Statistical Bulletin Education Series Edn/B1/2006/1: Pupils in Scotland, 2005,* http://www.scotland.gov.uk/Publications/2006/02/28083932/37

SG (Scottish Government) (2007b), *Statistics Publication Notice. Education and Training Series. Pre-School and Childcare Statistics 2007,* http://www.scotland.gov.uk/Resource/Doc/198709/0053102.pdf

Teese, R. *et al.* (2006), *Spain Country Note - Equity in Education Thematic Review,* OECD, Paris.

The Poverty Site website (2007), "Educational attainment at age 11", http://www.poverty.org.uk/S14/index.shtml

Thorpe, G. (2004), *PISA 2003: Initial Report on Scotland's Performance in Mathematics, Science and Reading,* Scottish Executive, Edinburgh

UNDP (2006), *Human Development Report 2006,* United Nations Human Development Programme, http://hdr.undp.org/hdr2006/statistics/indicators/147.html

Willms, J. Douglas (2006), *Learning Divides: Ten Policy Questions about the performance and equity of schools and schooling systems*, UNESCO, Montreal.

3. The Comparative Performance of Scottish Schools

Scottish children achieve at a consistently high level in the Programme for International Student Assessment (PISA). This is true both over time (2000, 2003) and across the domains of mathematics, reading, and science (Thorpe, 2004; SEED, 2007, App. J). This OECD report cannot examine PISA findings in detail in each of these domains. Rather the aim is to highlight certain aspects of the Scottish achievement profile which go beyond simple rank order in international league tables and which may help assess the underlying strengths of the nation's school system as well as the challenges it faces.

Scotland has both a high overall level of achievement in mathematics and a low proportion of under-achieving students. As observed in Chapter 2, only 3 in 100 students achieve at below Level 1. The number achieving at Level 1 is 9 in 100 (see Figure 3.1).

PISA is concerned with the ability of 15 year-olds to apply their mathematical knowledge—as distinct from mastery of the school curriculum as such. The concern is not with how well young people do in examinations in competition with each other or with the level of the curriculum at which they are assessed in examinations. PISA abstracts from the institutional framework of curriculum and assessment and looks only at how well learning is applied to real-world situations.

On this approach, the fact that only 12% of Scottish students under-achieve suggests that the program of studies in the compulsory years of secondary school works well. In other countries, which also operate comprehensive school systems, more than twice the proportion of 15 year-olds under-achieve and a smaller proportion achieve at high levels (*e.g.*, Spain, the United States).

This finding implies that the Scottish school system is more equitable *as regards student competencies*. It is not necessarily more equitable in the ways in which learning is formally examined or the level of the curriculum to which students have access or the qualifications they are awarded or the pathways they take. These relate to the way institutional arrangements work, and these arrangements do not work equally well for all children and young people. However, on the basis of PISA results, it could be inferred that access to good opportunities to learn is broadly and effectively open. Whatever the ways in which Scottish students are classified, graded and ranked in the "vocabulary" of their own system, a high proportion are able to use their mathematical knowledge well and few have very poor skills.

Figure 3.1 Distribution of students by level of mathematical literacy, 2003

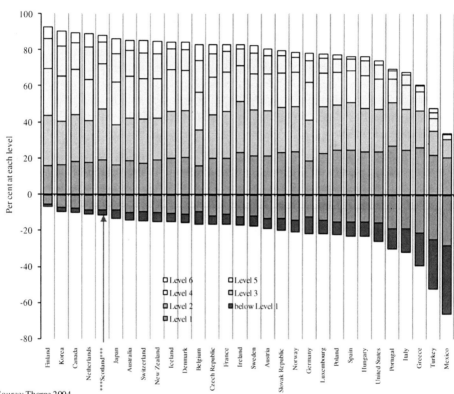

Source: Thorpe 2004

Scotland is a leading nation on these measures. To capture this, Figure 3.2 compares participating countries on two dimensions: the mean score on the mathematics literacy scale (*horizontal axis*) and the per cent of 15 year-olds who are under-achieving (*vertical scale*).

Figure 3.2 Mean score in mathematical literacy and per cent of low achievers, 2003

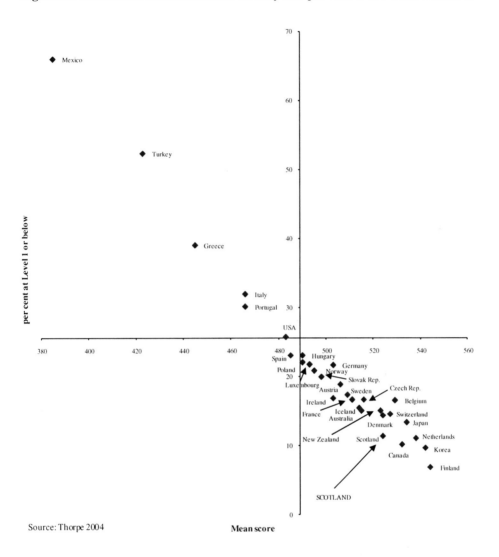

Source: Thorpe 2004

Countries with high average scores and below-average percentages of low achievers are found in the fourth quadrant (*lower right*). They are bunched together because of the extreme values on both scales of Mexico and Turkey. From one point of view, this compression of most of the developed nations in the OECD into an apparently narrow range of "high achievement" is misleading, or there is considerable variation in the group.

Scotland, for example, is well above most European nations on its mean score in mathematics and also has proportionately only half as many low achievers as Spain, Hungary, or Poland.

But while mainly-European nations do differ significantly from the OECD country mean, the extent to which they do so is eclipsed by the great distances separating them from developing nations, such as Mexico and Turkey, and even some European nations (Greece, Italy, Portugal).

It is helpful to keep Scotland's relative position in perspective. It does occupy an advanced position against its main trading competitors. But in world terms, little separates it from most of them. Without a continuing strong emphasis on the twin objectives of equity *and* quality, Scotland could slip through the ranks. It could be bypassed economically and become more divided socially. Its population might be less well-prepared to manage the demands of a global economy and the industry, occupational and productivity changes that must occur to assure a high standard of living, social cohesion, and the moral well-being of all of its people. The task is not to maintain a high educational ranking for its own sake, but to meet national economic, social and cultural objectives.

Scotland's challenge: making good schools more accessible and effective

The capacity of Scotland to maintain its strong position internationally presents a distinctive challenge by comparison with some of the OECD nations whose performance exceeds it or approximates it. Scotland has a comprehensive system of secondary schools. There is less variation in student performance in Scotland than in all other OECD nations, except Finland (SEED, 2007, App. J). Relatively little of the difference in student achievement that is observed is attributable to how **schools** differ. This contrasts with a country, like the Netherlands, which outperforms Scotland, but much of whose difference in student achievement is due to variation **between schools** (over 50% compared to only 10% in the case of Scotland).

Figure 3.3 compares countries by the proportion of variation in student achievement attributable to how schools differ and the proportion due to how individuals differ.

Figure 3.3 Between-school and within-school variation in mathematics performance

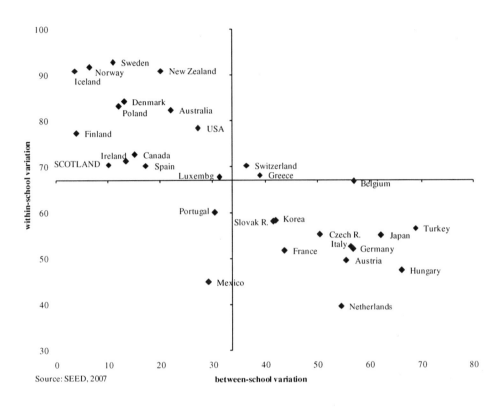

Source: SEED, 2007

What this means for Scotland is that sustainability and improvement in performance hinge much more than in countries such the Netherlands, Austria, Germany or France on tackling the factors that prevent children and young people from gaining the most benefit from an excellent school system. The problem is not, in the main, unequal access to good schools—as if there were wide variations in school quality—but unequal capacity to use good schools well.

This inference must be treated with care. Not all schools work equally well in Scotland. But the gaps between them are far less important than differences between students. In Scotland, **who you are** is far more important than **what school you attend**. But the fact that it *does* matter who you are also says that the school system as a whole is not strong enough to make this not matter.

The influence of socio-economic status on mathematics performance

As in other OECD countries, the big factor that impedes the ability of Scottish children to use school effectively is socio-economic status. This factor is more complex than poverty. Socio-economic status relates to cultural attributes and practices—family values, child rearing, language development, health and physical well-being, aspirations—and also financial capacity (for an overview, see Field, Kuczera, and Pont, 2007; Teese, 2007a).

However, the influence of socio-economic status (SES) does not lie simply in the set of negative or positive presenting characteristics of individuals. The reason why these characteristics matter is because the cognitive and cultural demands made by school act unequally on children and must be balanced by appropriate measures of support. This support may be too weak, for example, through lack of good quality pre-school provision, poor supervision of health and welfare in primary school, inadequate individual attention, teaching that is undifferentiated, and curriculum that is insensitive to context and capacity. The high concentration of social need in some regions and schools multiplies individual problems, for example, through negative peer effects and parental malaise, while stretching the resources of schools to the limit. The influence of SES lies, not in individuals, but in relationships and settings. These are general observations rather than specific comments about Scotland.

In all the "high achieving/high equity" nations with which Scotland can be compared—Finland, Korea, Canada, the Netherlands, to name only the top ones—SES exercises more or less influence over student performance in PISA mathematics. In some of these nations, this influence is limited. For example, in both Canada and Finland, only about 11% of total variance is accounted for by SES. But in other nations, it is much higher, *e.g.*, the Netherlands (18.6%). Scotland lies at this point in the spectrum (18.1%). In other nations, SES exerts a still stronger influence, *e.g.*, France (20%), Germany (23%), Belgium (24%), Hungary (27%). But none of these nations performs as well as Scotland. It could be argued that the influence of SES is holding them back from a more consistently high performance as is the much greater weight of "between school" factors that is true of all of them. The challenge for Scotland is how to maintain its high overall level of performance, while substantially improving the capacity of poorer children to benefit from school.

One measure of the extent of this challenge is given by how well low SES students in Scotland compare to high SES students. There is a considerable gap in mean scores between these two groups—482 for the lowest SES quarter compared to 573 for the highest SES quarter (SEED,

2007d, App. J). How does this compare with other OECD countries, and more particularly with the nine leading countries against which Scotland can be usefully benchmarked?

Figure 3.4 shows that the gap between rich and poor in Scotland is average for the comparator group. Some countries have bigger gaps, *e.g.*, Belgium, and to a much lesser extent, the Netherlands and New Zealand. Others have much smaller gaps, notably Canada and Finland. But it is also clear from the chart that young people from the lowest SES backgrounds in Scotland perform well below their peers in the Netherlands, Korea, Canada and Finland. In the last two countries, low SES students perform much better **and** there is also a much smaller gap between them and high SES students. This is not because young people from the most well-educated homes in Canada or Finland achieve at lower levels than in other comparator countries. The smaller social gap is due to better performance of young people from less well-educated and poorer families. This is where Scotland needs to improve by comparison with other leading OECD nations.

Figure 3.4 Mathematics scores of low SES students and gap between low and high SES students, Scotland and benchmarking countries, 2003

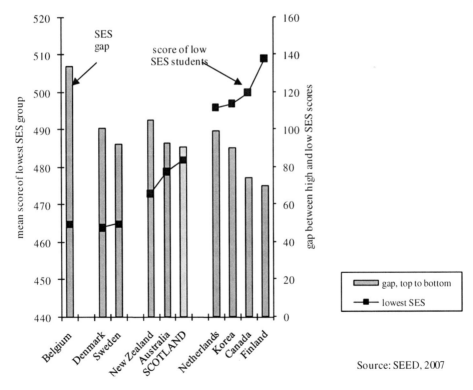

Source: SEED, 2007

Social differences in reading performance

A similar challenge exists in reading. The performance of young people from the lowest SES homes in Scotland is clearly superior to that of their social peers in several comparator nations—Belgium and Denmark. However, it is inferior to the Netherlands, Australia, Canada, Korea, and Finland. In four of these countries, the performance of students from the highest SES backgrounds is also superior to Scotland. Whether the sometimes-small differences in average scores which decide the rank of a country in these comparisons are statistically significant is one thing. But the gaps between rich and poor are the main concern. In Scotland, as in other comparator nations, these are large.

Within the comparator group of nations, Korea, Canada and Finland are outstanding in minimizing the social gap through higher performance by low SES students, while maintaining above-average performance by high SES students. Figure 3.5 shows that, in reading, Scotland is some way behind these leaders. The performance of both its low SES and its high SES students is only about average for the comparator group.

The countries that have done most to reduce the social gap in student performance can point to a comparatively limited influence of socio-economic status on achievement. In Korea, Canada and Finland, socio-economic status accounts for between 9.92% and 10.91% of the variation in reading scores. In Scotland, the influence of SES is much stronger—almost twice as high. It accounts for 19% of reading variation (and 18% of mathematics variation, as observed earlier).

The strong performance of Scotland on PISA mathematics and reading achievement thus needs to be qualified. Within Scottish schools, young people from low SES backgrounds encounter barriers which keep their performance well below that of socially more advantaged students. The school system itself is not divided into sites of very unequal quality and opportunity. Rather it is the relationship of schools in their generality to children from less well-educated and poor families that is problematic. This makes the goal of tackling low achievement more elusive and seemingly intractable. The barriers are embedded in the normal ways in which schools tend to work—schools independently assessed as generally good or very good.

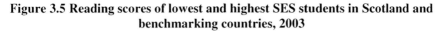

Figure 3.5 Reading scores of lowest and highest SES students in Scotland and benchmarking countries, 2003

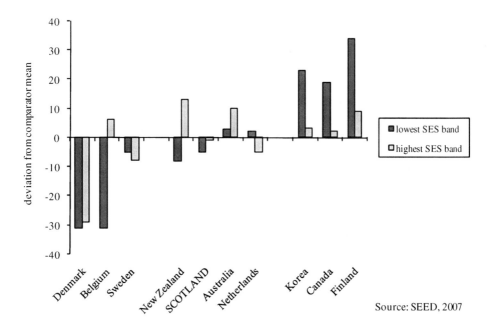

Source: SEED, 2007

Curriculum, teaching emphasis and style, the values and expectations of teachers, the level of individual support and supervision, the quality of the teaching resources available in particular classrooms—it is through all these ways that schools relate to families. And this relationship is more or less favourable, depending on the values, language skills, attitudes to learning, and health and well-being of children from socially different homes and neighbourhoods.

Formal equity may mask social disadvantage

The disadvantages experienced in school by children from less well-educated and poorer families tend to be obscured when schools are generally well-resourced and equipped. Formal equity means that class-sizes and student-teacher ratios do not vary from school to school, that all pupils have access to the same level and quality of teaching resources, and that there are no great differences in facilities and also in support services. Fairness in these terms may give rise to the impression that schools relate equally well to children from all social backgrounds, especially when the social differences between children themselves are more subtle and not very marked or overt. In such contexts, any differences in student achievement will likely be attributed to individual factors or blamed on families who are seen as failing to take advantage of good chances created for all children.

By comparison with other OECD countries, Scotland has favourable student-teacher ratios, a high proportion of fully certified teachers, and a markedly high proportion of teachers with an ISCED 5A qualification (SEED, 2007, App. J). Teaching resources in the field of mathematics present a more mixed, but generally favourable picture as well. On the surface, equity seems to be served.

How principals see the educational resources in their schools

The assessment of a school's educational resources made by principals as part of the PISA survey confirms the formally equitable character of Scottish education. Principals across the OECD were asked to rate the adequacy of a school's resources from a teaching point of view. Resources include instructional materials, computers, software for teaching, instructional calculators, library materials, audio-visual resources, and science laboratory equipment and materials. An index of quality of educational resources was constructed from responses.

On this index, Scottish secondary schools are amongst the most well-resourced in the OECD. The mean score on quality of educational resources places Scotland equal second to the United States and Switzerland and exceeded only by Korea and Australia. Scottish headteachers, though, are not uniformly positive, and there remains a large gap between schools judged to have a high standard of instructional materials, equipment and technology and those judged to have a low standard. However, the least well resourced schools in Scotland are still judged better by a considerable margin than the poorest in the OECD, and better than almost all of Scotland's comparator nations. Also, the most well-resourced schools in Scotland are evidently better than those in almost all comparator nations (as reported in Figure 3.6).

The very positive assessments of resource quality in Scottish secondary schools would suggest that the origins of low achievement in mathematics are more complex and subtle than either access to formally qualified teachers or the level of educational materials, equipment and technology in schools. For Scotland, PISA points away from the qualifications of teachers, student-teacher ratios, and instructional technology and materials to the dimensions of curriculum, instructional context and process—dimensions more difficult to measure, but more weighty in impact.

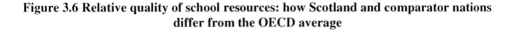

Figure 3.6 Relative quality of school resources: how Scotland and comparator nations differ from the OECD average

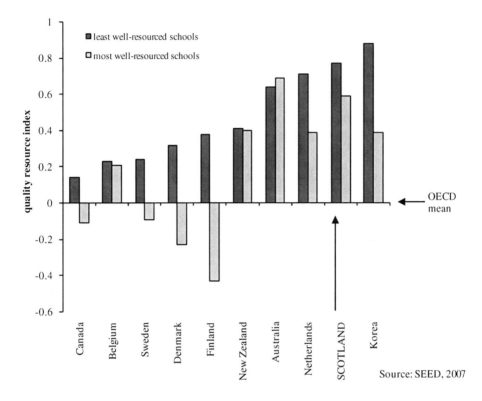

Source: SEED, 2007

How mathematics students see their classes

The views of students themselves as gathered in the PISA survey suggest weaknesses in the instructional context and process as one source of under-achievement in mathematics that is more likely to affect young people from low SES backgrounds.

In 2003, students were asked to comment on the frequency with which (a) their classmates did not listen to the teacher, (b) there was noise and disorder, (c) students took a long time to settle down, (d) students could not work well, and (e) it took a long time for students to start working. Responses to these items were combined into a single index of disciplinary climate.

Scottish students generally offer favourable assessments of the behaviour of their classmates in mathematics classrooms. The best classes in Scotland receive a higher score on the disciplinary climate index than the best classes in OECD countries on average. So, too, do the next best classes, and the next best below them. It is only the worst classes in Scotland that receive a rating below the average for the worst classes in the OECD as a whole, and this indicates only a marginally greater dissatisfaction (see Figure 3.7).

Figure 3.7 Scotland and the OECD country average on the index of disciplinary climate in mathematics classrooms

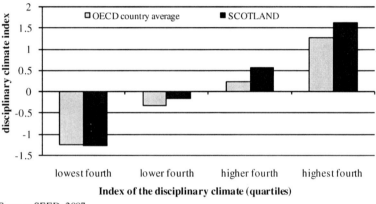

Source: SEED, 2007

From one perspective, this is a positive finding. Scottish students are on the whole more positive than their peers in most other countries. But from another perspective, the classroom climate findings of PISA are disturbing. There is a large gap between the best and the worst classes in mathematics. This gap is larger in Scotland than in any of the comparator nations (Figure 3.8).

However, it is not the comparative size of the gap between best and worst classrooms that is the most disturbing, but the impact this has on **student achievement**. As the disciplinary climate in mathematics classes weakens, there is also a fall in achievement. This can be seen in Figure 3.9 which compares mean student performance from the most favourable to the least favourable classes as ranked by students. Notice that Scotland's worst-judged schools have the lowest ranking of comparator nations, while the change in rating from the worst-judged to the best-judged is the steepest in Scotland.

Figure 3.8 Gap between best and worst mathematics classrooms: deviations from the OECD average for comparator nations and Scotland

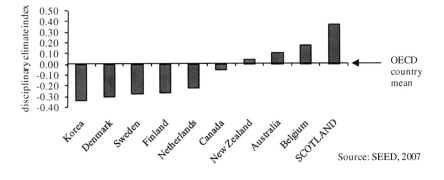

Source: SEED, 2007

Figure 3.9 Mean student achievement in best and worst classrooms: comparator nations and Scotland

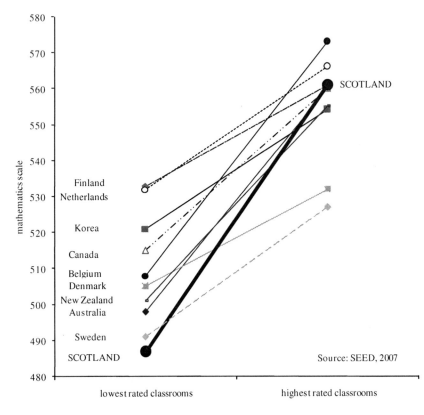

The unevenness in the climate of mathematics classrooms in Scottish high schools favours more highly achieving students. Superiority in the disciplinary climate of mathematics classrooms comes at the expense of weaker learners. Scotland is, in effect, harder on them than are other countries.

Failure to achieve more consistency in the climate of mathematics classrooms is captured in the statistic that measures how much of the variation in student performance is accounted for by change in disciplinary climate. For the OECD, the figure is 3.4%. For Scotland, it is three times higher (10.51%). This is far and away the biggest impact of disciplinary climate of any OECD country. Account taken of the large standard error associated with this estimate, the picture is still one suggestive of a strong academic emphasis across Scottish high schools, favouring high attaining students, and considerable dissonance in classrooms where the demands of the mathematics curriculum are much more difficult to meet and where the experience of failure is much more common.

Conclusion

Scotland's high overall achievements in mathematics, reading and science, and the comparatively small proportion of low achievers in these learning domains bears out the strengths of its comprehensive schools. So, too, does the fact that very little of the variation in student achievement is due to how schools differ. Scotland has succeeded in building a widely accessible and high quality system of secondary schools which are shared by most families as a community asset. PISA findings confirm the generally very positive assessments of HMIE.

However, not all Scottish children and young people enjoy equitable access to this fine school system. The profile of mathematical competency which shows that only 12 in 100 students achieve poorly (Figure 3.1) conceals the social patterns running through this. The social mix of achievers at each level of competency varies. Fewer young people from the poorest family backgrounds are found at the highest level (Level 6), while on the other hand they are over-represented at lower levels. Most of the variation in student achievement in Scotland is due to "within school" factors—that is, to the way individuals differ. Who you are matters a great deal more in Scotland than what school you attend, and "who you are" is defined largely in terms of socio-economic status.

Scottish society is not highly stratified in social terms and its schools are not highly segregated. So learning gaps are seen as primarily linked to poverty and deprivation. This turns attention away from the more diffuse cultural differences associated with family educational, occupational and income levels (socio-economic status). These differences are relational. They concern both the qualities of individuals (values, attitudes, behaviours) *and* the action of institutions (what schools demand and how they work). While a focus on deprivation is extremely important, it should not be so exclusive as to screen out the relational factors of socio-economic status. For without bringing these into view, little progress will be made in reducing the impact of a set of factors which, on PISA tests, account for around a fifth of the variation in mathematics, reading and science achievement.

The survey findings from PISA confirm that secondary schools are generally well-staffed, with favourable student-teacher ratios and trained teachers, including in areas, like mathematics, where shortages can sometimes be acute. Scottish headteachers report that secondary schools are well supplied with educational materials, equipment and technology. Differences in access to these contribute little to measured differences in student achievement. Equity, in the formal sense of an equal distribution of human and physical resources, is a strong point in Scottish school education.

To explain why students from different social backgrounds achieve unequally well requires investigating other factors, notably curriculum, the teaching context, and instructional processes. Quality of instructional experience, as captured in the PISA index of disciplinary climate, is quite variable in Scotland. It is associated with a large range in student achievement. This highlights the relational nature of factors which contribute to inequality. Poor climate in a mathematics class is an issue of curriculum as well as teaching, and of peer effects as well as individual attributes. The worst classes in Scotland are almost certainly not a socially random sample of all mathematics classes.

PISA reveals major strengths—comprehensive schools, wide access to high-quality environments for learning, overall effectiveness in learning outcomes, well-resourced and equipped schools. But PISA also points to some big challenges. How can Scotland extend the benefits of good schooling to a wider range of children and young people? What does it need to do to reduce the barriers to successful learning which are embedded in curriculum and teaching practice in **good**—not bad schools?

International measures of student competency help focus attention on weaknesses in the performance of otherwise very effective school systems. But to identify the barriers to greater and more equitable success requires analysis of **institutional** measures—a report card written in the national "vocabulary" of curriculum and qualifications, tests and examinations, and one that looks at differences inside a national system which are largely inaccessible to international surveys. The next chapter turns to this task.

References

Field, S., Kuczera, M. and B. Pont (2007). *No More Failures: Ten Steps to Equity in Education,* OECD, Paris

OECD (2001), *Knowledge and Skills for Life,* Organisation for Economic Co-operation and Development, Paris.

Scottish Executive Education Department (2007), *OECD Review of the Quality and Equity of Education Outcomes in Scotland: Diagnostic Report,* available on the OECD website http://dx.doi.org/10.1787/148012367602 or www.oecd.org/edu/reviews/nationalpolicies.

Teese, R. (2007a), "Time and space in the reproduction of educational inequality" in Teese, R., Lamb, S. and M. Duru-Bellat (eds.), *International Studies in Educational Inequality, Theory and Policy*: *Vol. 3,* pp. 1-21, Springer, Dordrecht.

Thorpe, G. (2004), *PISA 2003: Initial Report on Scotland's Performance in Mathematics, Science and Reading,* Scottish Executive, Edinburgh.

4. The Achievement Gap in Scottish School Education

In this chapter, the OECD review team takes a national perspective on how well Scottish schools work. Data from national surveys and from examinations are drawn on to describe achievement patterns and to highlight the processes that prevent a more consistently high performance in student learning. In Scotland, examinations play a large role in the provision of compulsory schooling, and it is appropriate to pay close attention to patterns and trends in student results.

PISA findings demonstrate that Scottish schools are highly competitive internationally. But they also show that the experience of success could be more widely shared. This would require reducing the impacts of poverty and low socio-economic status. But how do these factors work in the Scottish context?

International research points to the characteristics of families and neighbourhoods, on the one side, and curriculum, classsrooms, teachers and teaching, on the other. The interactions between these factors lead to an achievement gap that widens over the stages of schooling. Weaker learners are progressively excluded—they are often from poorer backgrounds— while stronger ones, usually from more educated families, are promoted. Is this the pattern in Scotland? If so, are schools tackling the points which an analysis of achievement patterns would suggest as most salient?

Children ahead and children behind

National assessments of student learning confirm the strengths of Scottish education exhibited in PISA. In the Scottish Survey of Achievement (SSA), every second child in Primary 3 is one year ahead in reading (Level B instead of Level A) (Figure 4.1a, from SEED, 2006s).

Nearly 1 in 4 are between two and three years ahead for they are reading well at the level expected of Primary 6 pupils. Similarly, amongst Primary 5 pupils, every fourth child is assessed as "very good" or "well established" in reading at Level D. This is the standard expected of Primary 7 pupils.

Figure 4.1a Attainment at different levels of reading, P3 to S2 (%)

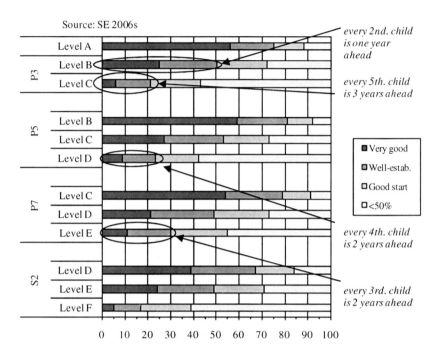

These positive signs are balanced by some negative ones. Looking again at children in P5, every fifth is at least one year behind (not "well established" at the expected level for P4). This is also approximately the situation amongst P7 pupils—about 1 in 5 are at least one year behind. This gap widens by the second year of secondary school. For over 30% of S2 students are not "well established" at the level expected in P7 (Figure 4.1b).

The pursuit of high standards is necessary if Scotland is to prepare its children to contribute on the world stage to economic and social well-being. Their capacity to contribute will be reflected in a consistently high performance in international assessments of student learning. But a high standard should come from across the country and operate as an objective which brings the country together, ensuring that no child misses out.

To give this objective practical sense requires an emphasis on students who are under-achieving. This is not to ignore the needs of high achievers, but rather to focus national efforts on the most vulnerable groups, for whom the first problem is the lack of an integrated view within education of the origins of under-achievement, and the second, a lack of expectations. This is the focus recommended by HMIe (2006m, section 4).

Figure 4.1b Attainment at different levels of reading, P5 to S2 (%)

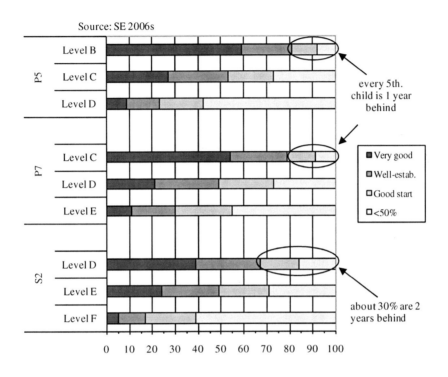

The achievement gap over stages of schooling

The objective of a consistently high performance contributed by all children across the country requires ongoing monitoring and investigation of quality of learning and participation within the curriculum. Findings from the National Survey of 5-14 Achievement Levels (a programme which ceased in 2004 and was replaced by the SSA) confirm the widening achievement gap amongst children from at least P6.

For example, in the school year 2003/04, around 15% of P6 pupils were assessed as not reaching the expected Level C in reading. This rose to 26% of pupils not reaching the expected Level D in P7 and 36% not reaching Level E in Secondary 2 (SE 2004a). It is possible that such improvements reflect more test-oriented teaching, but the OECD review team is not in a position to assess this and has not seen evidence in relation to it.

Balancing this pattern is a clear trend to improvement over time from the 2000/01 school year. Attainment in mathematics illustrates this trend. Generally speaking, each year over the period to 2003/04 brought an increase in the proportions of pupils at each stage achieving the level of mathematics expected of them. For example, while as many as 49% of Secondary 2 pupils were assessed as not reaching Level E in mathematics in 2000/01, this fell to 41% by the last year of the National Survey (SEED, 2004a). Figure 4.2 shows both the widening achievement gap over stages of schooling and the trend to improvement in recent years. A similar pattern of improving standards was also recorded in reading and writing.

Figure 4.2 Mathematics attainment from 2000/01 to 2003/04 by stage of schooling (%)

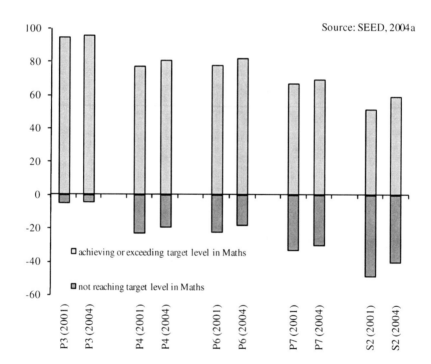

Important as these improving trends are, the evidence points to a continuing gap in achievement which widens over the later years of primary school and into the early years of secondary school. In 2003/04, as many as 41% of S2 pupils were assessed as not reaching Level E in mathematics.

The widening achievement gap was experienced both by boys and girls, though to different degrees, depending on curriculum area. For example, about 30 in 100 girls in S2 did not meet expected standards in reading in 2003/04, while the figure for boys was much higher (41%). In mathematics, S2 boys also under-performed girls at Level E (42.3% compared to 38.7%).

The gap between regions of Scotland

At any given stage of schooling, there are also gaps between different groups of children, between schools, and between local authorities. The limited sampling coverage of the Scottish Survey of Achievement does not provide a complete picture of achievement gaps, particularly across and within different regions within Scotland. A fuller picture is available from the former National Survey. This reveals very considerable variations across local authorities, though care must be taken with the estimates, owing to issues of quality control. To take extremes, just over 75 in 100 S2 students in East Dunbartonshire attained Level E in reading in 2003/04 compared to only 54 in 100 in Glasgow City. The wide range in under-achievement across local authorities is displayed in Figure 4.3 (SEED, 2004a).

Geographical patterns in under-achievement reflect the influence of social area factors, such as urban poverty or deprivation, low socio-economic status, and health and well-being factors which affect child development and learning. Depth of deprivation is a strong predictor of under-achievement. Amongst Secondary 2 students, under-achievement in reading nearly doubles from East Dunbartonshire (24%) to Glasgow City (46%). Deprivation, as measured by a local authority's national share of the 20% most deprived zones (SE, 2006g), explains about 29% of the variation in under-achievement ($r = .535$) (see Figure 4.4).

Researchers have pointed to the limited degree of social segregation in Scottish schools (Croxford and Raffe, 2005, p. 5). Comprehensive schools, which have broad social intakes, are a major vehicle of equity and of high national standards of achievement as well. They represent a key strength of Scottish education. However, residential differentiation—identified as the main source of social segregation among Scottish schools (Paterson, 2001)— may weaken the potential of a comprehensive system, unless systemic counter-active measures are taken. The close relationship between depth of deprivation and under-achievement points to the action of social processes which concentrate disadvantage in certain regions, leaving others relatively free of this.

Figure 4.3 Under-achievement in reading at S2 by local authority, 2003/04 (%)

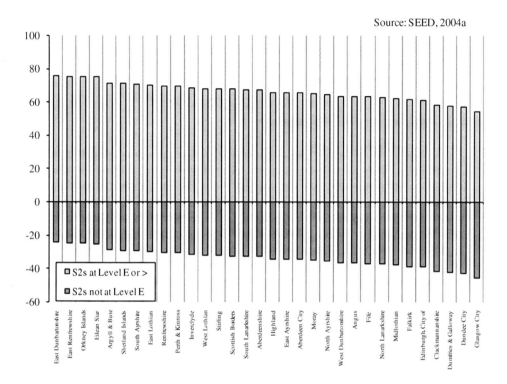

Source: SEED, 2004a

Over half of the most disadvantaged areas in Scotland are concentrated in just four local authorities—Glasgow City, North Lanarkshire, Fife, and South Lanarkshire. These enrol nearly a third of all Secondary 2 pupils (30%) (see Figure 4.5) (enrolment shares are derived from SE, 2003p). Rates of under-achievement in these local authorities therefore have major significance for Scotland as a whole.

Glasgow City, North Lanarkshire, and Fife all have rates of under-achievement which are above the national average. The largest local authority—Glasgow City—has a very high concentration of deprivation (29% of all severely deprived zones), enrols 9% of the S2 population, and has a rate of under-achievement of about 48% (far above the national average).

Almost every second child in S2 in Glasgow City under-achieves in reading (and high proportions also have difficulties in writing and mathematics). The position in North Lanarkshire is much better in terms of under-achievement, with the rate only about 3-4 percentage points higher than the national average (compared to 12 percentage points higher in Glasgow City). Nevertheless this rate concerns 7% of the total S2 population in Scotland. Fife is in a very similar position.

Figure 4.4 Deprivation level and under-achievement in S2 Reading by Local Authority, 2003/04

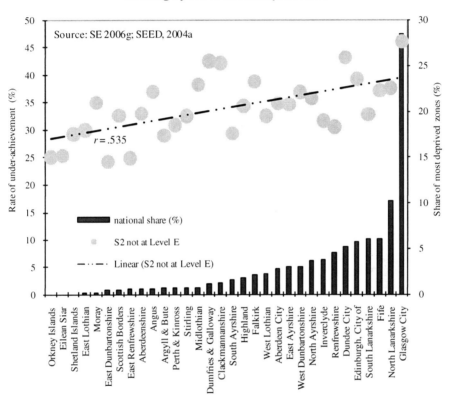

The relationship between **share of disadvantage** and **rate of under-achievement** is far from consistent or linear. Some local authorities have only a small share of disadvantage, but still record very high levels of under-achievement (*e.g.*, Clackmannanshire, Dumfries and Galloway). Some local authorities, on the other hand, have fairly large shares of deprivation, but below-average under-achievement (South Lanarkshire, Renfrewshire, Inverclyde). This could be because disadvantage is highly concentrated in certain areas **within each local authority,** and its effects are swamped by good performance in more mixed or upmarket areas in the same local authority.

Figure 4.5 Local authority shares of S2 students and most deprived zones (%)

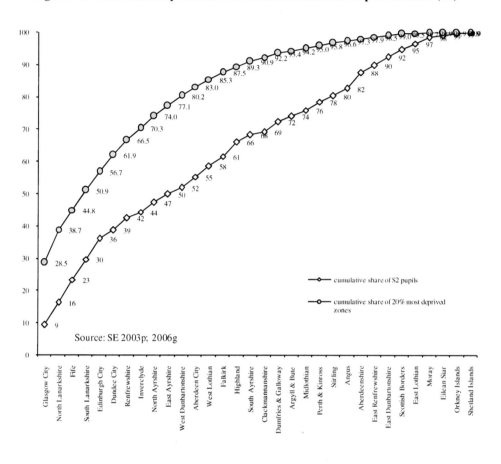

However, there are clear differences at extremes. At one end are local authorities which, as a group, contain a very large share of total deprivation and also quite a large share of total enrolments. In general, these local authorities have high rates of under-achievement. Nearly 40% of total S2 pupils attend schools in six local authorities, five of which have above-average or well above-average rates of under-achievement (see Figure 4.6).

At the opposite end of the spectrum are local authorities which have very little measured deprivation, but only a small share of total enrolments. In almost all cases, the rates of under-achievement in these local authorities are below average for Scotland, and usually far below (between 8 and 10 percentage points). However, this strong performance relates only to a very modest share of total S2 enrolments and consequently has less impact on the national picture than the high rates of under-achievement recorded in those local authorities which are both large and poor.

Figure 4.6 Local authority shares of most deprived zones and all S2 students, and rates of under-achievement in reading

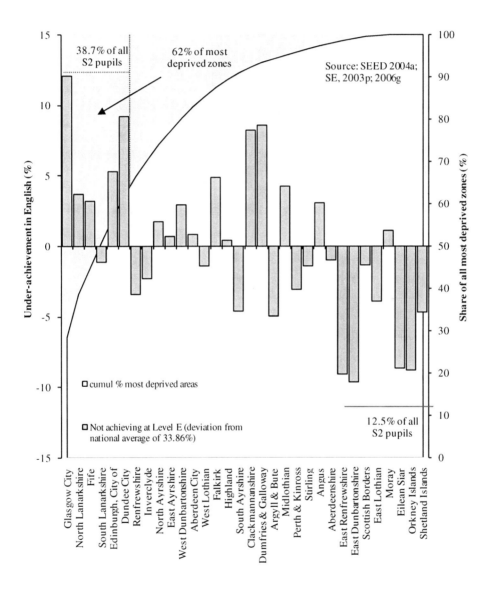

Uneven achievement at the end of compulsory school

The achievement gap which widens during primary and early secondary education lays the basis for unequal attainment at the end of compulsory school. Over the last decade, there has been continuing improvement in Standard Grades (or equivalents) for Scottish pupils on average. But there has been very little improvement amongst the weakest learners. The gap between them and the average pupil is very large and persistent (Figure 4.7, from SEED, unpublished tables).

The size of this gap should be seen in the context of the differentiated structure of the S3-S4 curriculum. This allows pupils to sit for exams at different (and multiple) levels of difficulty. In theory, this should moderate achievement gaps by allowing pupils to advance at different rates in different areas of the curriculum and to have their learning assessed at appropriate levels. Despite this provision, there is a large and persistent divergence in achievement as measured by tariff scores[2].

Figure 4.7 Gap between the average pupil and the low achiever in S4, 1996 to 2006

Source: SE unpublished tables

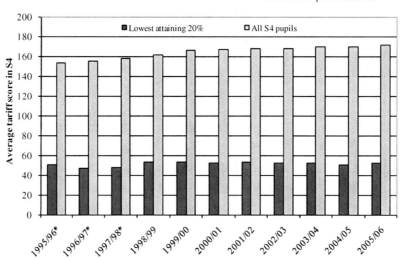

---

[2]   Tariff scores—attainment data may be presented as average tariff scores to enable certification of different types to be considered together. This makes it easier to compare average attainment for different sub-groups within the population. The tariff score of a pupil is calculated by allocating a score to each level of qualification and award, using the Unified Points Score scale. For example, a Standard Grade at level 1 counts as 38 points and at level 4 counts as 14 points. See SEED, 2007i.

Weakening relationships: absences and exclusions

The causes of under-achievement in school are complex. From a teacher's perspective, the most visible influences are the values, attitudes and capacities of parents. Schools serving poorer areas sometimes have to manage multiple kinds of disadvantage. A pupil's relationship to school may be a fragile one, as evident in patterns of attendance and absence.

In the 15% most deprived areas of Scotland, average attendance in publicly-funded primary schools in 2003/04 accounted for 93% of time, with 6.9% representing absences (either authorized or unauthorized) and 0.05% representing temporary exclusions (SE, 2005s)[3].

More time was lost in the most deprived areas than in the rest of Scotland. While the gap was small, it is suggestive of the early onset of difficulties faced by schools in deprived areas in seeking to build positive relationships to school. In secondary school, the amount of time lost due to absences in these areas rose sharply from 6.9% (primary school) to 14.7%. This was very much higher than the 8.4% recorded for the rest of Scotland. Figure 4.8 reports pupil absence in terms of percentages of half-days lost by 1/20th. bands of multiple deprivation. This is done separately for primary and secondary school.

Figure 4.8 Pupil absence: all school pupils, 2003/4 by deprivation level

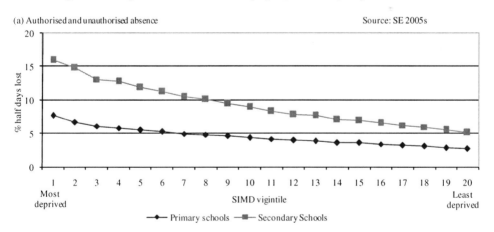

(a) Authorised and unauthorised absence   Source: SE 2005s

---

[3] From Table 5.9; the text accompanying this table in the original appears to refer to the wrong columns in the table.

The trend line which shows that absences grow as deprivation rises is more acute in the case of secondary school students. This points to the mounting difficulty experienced by secondary schools in building and sustaining positive relationships to school, and the greater difficulty experienced by parents in helping their children. As one headteacher explained to the OECD review team, the achievement gap "peaks when parents can't help any longer".

The increasing fragility of relationships is captured even more starkly when temporary exclusions are analysed by relative deprivation of social area. Figure 4.9 (from SE, 2005s) shows a trend to more exclusions in primary school in the most deprived areas.

Figure 4.9 Temporary exclusions, 2003/4 by deprivation level

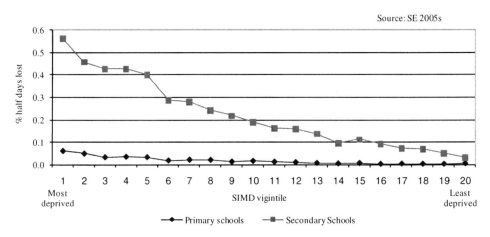

Source: SE 2005s

While temporary exclusions are rare in primary school, they occur with increasing frequency as deprivation worsens. The trend in secondary school is, however, quite marked. Scotland's most deprived areas contributed a total of 15.2% of total half-days in attendance in 2003/04, but as much as a third of all time lost through temporary exclusions, *i.e.*, about twice the share that might be expected.

Relationship to the curriculum

The tendency for absences and temporary exclusions to worsen sharply from primary to secondary school reflects, in part, the development cycle of the growing independence of adolescents. But it also reflects the greater challenge presented to young people of a curriculum which is more specialized, more intellectually demanding, and delivered in more academic and subject-centred settings.

In the early years of secondary school, pupils enter an environment where there is more pressure on them as individuals, where there is less group work (sharing of learning tasks), where parents can offer less direct instructional support, and where learning is eventually assessed through formal examinations. Added to the greater conceptual depth at which pupils have to work are the demands of tests which compare performance. The curriculum is split into different subject areas, with the attendant risks of a fragmentary view of the child and greater difficulty in addressing individual needs and preventing a slide in morale, engagement and achievement.

The impact of these changes in the environment of learning demands can be gauged from the weakening levels of pupil confidence in studying mathematics. TIMSS findings show that Scottish pupils in the fifth year of primary school have very high levels of confidence (SEED, 2006s). Almost 2 in 3 agree "a lot" that they are confident in studying mathematics. By the second year of secondary school, however, this measure of agreement has fallen to just over 1 in 2. Part of the loss is due to a rising proportion of pupils reporting a lack of confidence (from 11% in P5 to 15% in S2) (see Figure 4.10).

Figure 4.10 Confidence in mathematics from P5 to S2

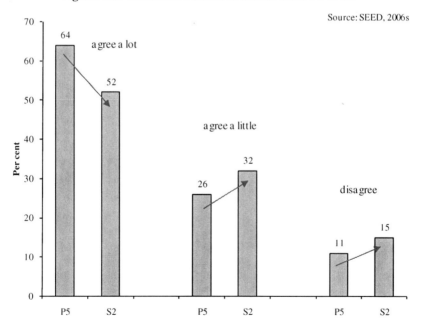

Source: SEED, 2006s

Confidence falls throughout the later stages of primary and into secondary school, and does not fall uniformly in all subject areas. Nor does it necessarily imply increasing failure. However, findings from other Scottish surveys show that this is indeed occurring. Scottish pupils continue to work away at mathematics, despite some loss of confidence in their abilities. However, there is a very sharp fall in their *enjoyment* of mathematics. While every second pupil in P5 agrees "a lot" that mathematics is enjoyable, this measure plummets to a mere 18% by S2. Rejection of the idea that mathematics is enjoyable rises sharply from 24% to 42%. Maths, it appears, has become work (see Figure 4.11).

Again this does not imply that Scottish pupils cannot do the work, or do it well. But falling self-confidence and plummeting enjoyment are likely to be experienced very unequally in the school system and will contribute significantly to the incidence of failure and under-achievement. Some pupils can manage the transition from "play" to "work" very well. Others require extra support and differentiated teaching approaches to ensure that they do experience success and that they can manage the cognitive shift to more abstract, theoretical work, often done in the silence of their own study time.

Figure 4.11 Enjoyment of mathematics: decline from Primary 5 to Secondary 2

Source: SEED, 2006s

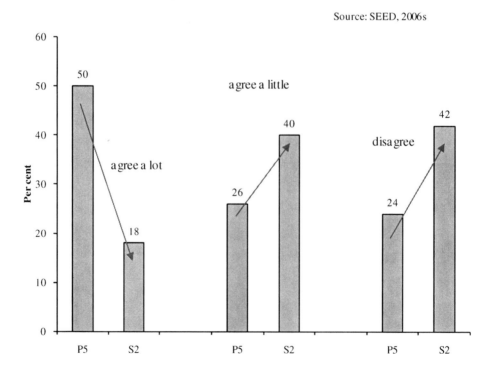

Incentives for learning

The growing maturity of young people as they complete the final years of compulsory school exposes the curriculum to questions of meaning and relevance. Students who have enjoyed a history of success are more protected from uncertainty about goals, purpose, and directions in the curriculum than those who have struggled. This protection is based partly on a firmer view of where they are heading—generally university—and partly on the manifest confidence that significant others have in them. University is an intermediate step between school and work and exercises an attractiveness and appeal in its own right, even in the absence of clear career goals. Because of this intrinsic appeal and recognized social value, university offers a sense of purpose to young people, and this throws a mantle of meaning over the subjects on which access to university most depends. This is notwithstanding the theoretical emphasis, limited obvious relevance, and abstraction of more 'academic' subjects. Successful learners can carry the load of abstraction more easily, thanks to the intermediate goal of university, which saves them from the need for early clarity and firmness about careers. Finally, university also crystallizes the broader benefits of education and culture—such as enjoyment of the arts and the pursuit of citizenship. These benefits have an institutional 'home' in university and other institutions of higher learning, which sanction them as socially valuable goals towards which schoolwork should be directed.

Scottish research finds that young people with a university goal relate more positively to the curriculum and also more broadly to the wider benefits of school (Careers Scotland, 2004). Conversely, those whose goals are much less clear and who do not have the advantage of a highly valued intermediate step to aim for have a weaker relationship to the school curriculum. Less successful students on the whole, they are more troubled by the curriculum in terms both of meaning and also the style of classroom learning which it demands. They want subjects in which they get to 'do' something, such as physical education (Careers Scotland, 2004). They want practical and group-based subjects and classroom activities of the kind they had in primary school. But, more than this, they want linkages between the world of school and the world of work.

This demand reflects the objectively greater weakness of their relationship to school. More often than not, they are low achievers and thus more likely to leave school early and enter the labour market. In the words of one teacher, "the lowest group are not keeping pace". Under-achievement in school is an **economic** risk, not only an academic or a cultural risk. Building a relationship to work through school addresses this risk. So the content of the curriculum will be viewed negatively when it fails to supply a bridge. There will be too few incentives—beginning with economic ones, but extending to the cultural benefits of attractive and engaging material and teaching. For it is just at the time when economic connections must be made to engage young learners that the curriculum becomes more specialized, conceptually demanding, and apparently inward-looking and detached from reality. Without incentives, interest flags and boredom sets in.

Low achievement and lack of motivation undermine the meaningfulness of compulsory schooling and pose a challenge to the Scottish system of differentiated levels of Standard Grades intended to ensure a satisfactory experience for all learners. Adjusting the cognitive level at which studies are attempted or examined does not in itself create strong incentives for student engagement. It may remove barriers. But it does not necessarily lift interest or give young people an experience of success or raise self-esteem to help with further study or employment.

The strategy of 'vertical' adjustment—lowering the cognitive demands on pupils—may in fact be less successful than a strategy of 'lateral' adjustment—broadening the range of studies and the types of learning that can be undertaken to boost levels of achievement in core skills.

Scottish teachers question whether the curriculum is able to support the whole spectrum of need. "We are currently tinkering with it...there's a range of things, but we haven't rethought the mainstream".

The upper secondary years

Without more progress in reducing the achievement gap in the compulsory years, pressure will continue to be placed on the operation of the National Courses in post-compulsory education. The structure of the curriculum in S5-S6 is also differentiated by levels—Access 1, Access 2, Access 3, Intermediate 1, Intermediate 2, Higher, Advanced Higher (SQA, 2006q). So that again, in theory, pupils can advance at a variable pace, with opportunities for all to proceed, regardless of prior achievement levels. But the evidence of the attainment of Scottish pupils in S5 and S6 indicates that both progression and attainment are significantly constrained by the uneven quality of learning experience in compulsory secondary education.

Low achievers have access to levels of study which were not available before the Higher Still reforms of the mid-1990s, but they nevertheless succeed at much lower rates than the average pupil, who in turn is less successful at differentiated levels of the curriculum than the high achiever, attempting mainly Highers or Advanced Highers (Raffe, Howieson and Tinklin, 2007). In short, the problems of achievement are carried forward rather than overcome. The relatively new structure of the 'climbing frame' both accommodates diversity and encourages aspirations, but does not close the gap of prior achievement.

While there has been an expansion of options, particularly for low to average students, and an increase in the number of courses which these students, in particular, have taken, the Higher Still reforms have not seen significant improvements in pass rates (Raffe, Howieson and Tinklin 2007). The reasons for this are complex. They include a gap in the capacity of students to manage external examinations as distinct from school assessments, a continuing lack of access to studies at an appropriate level, and transition difficulties in managing the workload and cognitive demand of Highers.

A falling-off of individual attention is reported by students—"there's been none of that this year"—just at the time when transition support is most needed. There is a much greater emphasis in S5 on individual learning. "To me," writes one student, "it was immediately apparent that 5th. year was going to ask more of me, and teachers all put an emphasis on the 'you' part." The heightened work pressures represented a "dramatic step up" for another student—accustomed to Credit grades—and the greater stress on personal responsibility for learning is typified by more class-free time as distinct from greater individual support.

These difficulties should be seen in the context of **rising attainment** in Standard Grades. There has been a strengthening of the platform in compulsory schooling, as reflected in the increased proportion of passes at Levels 1-2. But students still encounter significant problems of adaptation to the learning environment in the upper stages of secondary school, and the gaps between individuals are not reduced. The lowest achievers in S4 have much lower pass rates in S5, despite attempting courses at lower levels, and average students in S4 have lower pass rates than high achievers, also despite attempting courses at lower levels (Raffe, Howieson and Tinklin, 2007).

Taken together, these findings suggest that while Scottish students are achieving better results in compulsory school and enjoying wider access to the curriculum in post-compulsory school, under-achievement continues to hold back many. They are unable to convert better access into greater success. Gaps between individuals remain large, even after a third of the age-cohort has left school and differentiated opportunities have been created for continuing students.

Moreover, the weakest learners continue to be drawn disproportionately from poor families. Some stay on to qualify for a maintenance allowance, others because their parents know it is important, even if they themselves cannot help (and do not know the extent of the pressures on their children).

Parents may prefer school, even when their sons or daughters are struggling, because they see success at school as the only secure way forward that they themselves understand. Teachers do not always share this view. Some—and they may not be representative—feel that school is unsuitable and has little to offer students who have fallen behind. "There doesn't seem to be a place for them," an experienced teacher observes, "they should have gone on to further education...but there's a lot of pressure from parents." Contrasting with this view is the emphasis schools serving some of the poorest communities in Scotland place on regular attendance. They recognize that without building the relationship with families that this involves, the most disadvantaged children will be still further disadvantaged.

If we ignore the point at which young people leave school in Scotland, the divergence in qualifications obtained by those receiving free school meals and those who are not is quite striking. Fewer than 3 in 100 school leavers who are not receiving free meals obtain no qualification compared to 11 in 100 of those who do. About 15 in 100 school leavers from poor backgrounds obtain only two Level 4 passes and 12 in 100 only four Level 2 passes. By contrast, over 14% of school leavers who are not defined as in poverty pass two Level 6 courses and 13% pass two Level 7 courses. The impact of poverty on attainment is displayed in Figure 4.12 (from SEED, 2005q).

Figure 4.12 Qualifications of school leavers by poverty status (%)

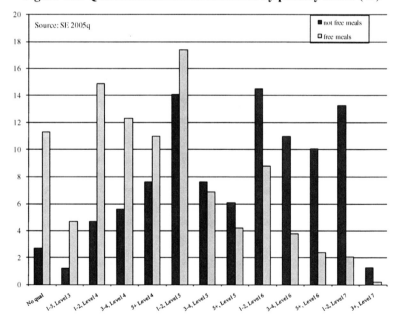

Conclusion

In this chapter, we have reviewed national findings on the performance of Scotland's schools. Our purpose has been to describe the variability in student achievement within a school system that performs highly by international standards. PISA provides information about a particular age-group—young people who, in Scotland, are reaching the end of compulsory school. National data from tests and examinations offer a wider angle. Along with the reports of HMIe, they show an achievement gap which widens over the stages of schooling, but especially during the later primary and compulsory secondary years.

During this critical phase, the progress of children, particularly in disadvantaged areas, tends to weaken. The transition from primary to secondary school is a shift in institutional setting which tests both the preparedness of children and the readiness of schools. Many children suffer a "dip". Change in setting is accompanied by growing complexity in the cognitive demands made on children. But at the same time there is a reduction in oversight of the whole child, thanks to the splintering of the teaching effort across different subjects. Teachers are trained to deliver subjects. They do not have cross-professional training, to quote an observation from a General Teaching Council forum, and in the past teachers were expected to be "passive", that is, instruments of the curriculum rather than carers of young learners.

Parents with limited formal education may disconnect from school during these years. They are less able to help and are also frequently less able to manage the tensions of children's adjustment to the secondary school environment. Communication between home and school greatly weakens. The pressure on children is to manage an increasing theoretical emphasis in their studies (*e.g.*, algebra) and to work more and more on their own. The shared and practical tasks of primary school give way to book-based and written assignments, intended to test and grade pupils (Teese and Polesel, 2003, Ch. 6). Confidence in mathematics and enjoyment in it fall away sharply as many children fail to make the cognitive shift required of success in secondary school.

A largely academic curriculum until recently has made few concessions to the need to see where school leads and why scholarly effort is important. More successful students enjoy greater certainty, and they can commit themselves more fully to schoolwork because there is a clear institutional goal: school leads to university. But for weaker learners, there is considerable uncertainty. If the curriculum offers no obvious economic incentives, engagement depends wholly on the intrinsic qualities of teachers and good teaching. But it is not necessarily the case that schools staff the most demanding classes with the best teachers, and the way resources are allocated across the whole programme of school may tend to favour the needs of students who also enjoy the greatest out-of-school support. "We can't cut class sizes in S2/S3 without starving S6 of specialist resources," one teacher says. Is this an issue in many Scottish high schools? It is an issue in at least one of Scotland's comparator nations (Lamb 2007).

The young people who are thought less likely to continue beyond the statutory leaving age present a continuing challenge to the culture of secondary schools. Notwithstanding a policy of broad participation in vocational studies for all young people, vocational education may be seen as particularly suited to the needs of less successful students, and vocational studies in turn seen as best provided in the setting of colleges. This creates a risk that both the curriculum and the pedagogical challenge are displaced and transferred, leaving the academic culture of the school intact. Students taking vocational options are the "Friday group—they feel there's greater maturity there [in the college] and they're moving on".

Vocational studies are seen mainly in terms of preparation for work and to make young people more employable. They are not seen as pedagogical and motivational tools to ease the cognitive shift by allowing an emphasis on applied learning, problem-solving and sharing of tasks. This weakens the framework of opportunities for children from poorer and less educated families, and they not unnaturally take refuge in a peer culture which reverses the tables and prides failure over success.

The processes of "inclusion" and "exclusion" which we have described are not unique to the Scottish context. One teacher felt that the S1/S2 "dip" was a Scottish problem. But in fact it is something shared by many systems, including the most high performing. In Scotland, a consistently high standard is expected of schools, not a trade-off between equity and quality.

Scottish schools are changing in what they teach, in instructional emphasis, in what teachers are encouraged to value and to expect, and in the quality of interactions between teachers and students (as exemplified in the willingness of some schools to solicit student views of teaching). The picture is less clear regarding how resources are used in schools at different stages of schooling and whether there is sufficient emphasis on the critical years of compulsory secondary education. Schools serving more educated families are under pressure to operate specialist academic programmes in S5 and S6, which in turn "absorb all resources", according to one teacher. Homogeneous intakes favour this strategy, as a headteacher observed. But what happens in more mixed settings, where many children are "behind the pace"?

Without significant cultural and organisational changes in schools, low achieving students will either have to leave school when they are legally free to do so or do as one caring headteacher recommends, "Just sing quietly, if you're no good".

Differences in motivation, attainment and aspirations crystallize in the qualifications which distinguish young people completing compulsory school and shape the range of destinations which they follow at the end of this stage. Chapter 5 examines trends and patterns in staying-on rates and post-school transition in Scotland.

References

Careers Scotland (2004), *Career Goals and Educational Attainment: What is the Link?* Careers Scotland, Glasgow.

Croxford, L. and D. Raffe (2005), "Secondary school organisation in England, Scotland and Wales since the 1980s", Paper for the seminar on Policy Learning in 14-19 Education, Joint Seminar of education and youth transitions Project and Nuffield review of 14 – 19 Education, 15 March 2005.

HMIe (2006m), *Missing Out: A report on children at risk of missing out on educational opportunities,* Her Majesty's Inspectorate of Education, Livingston.

Lamb, S. (2007), Three-year rolling benchmark in Victorian government schools. Unpublished research report for the Department of Education and Early Childhood Development (University of Melbourne, Centre for Post-Compulsory Education and Lifelong Learning).

Paterson, L. (2001), "Education and inequality in Britain", paper prepared for the social policy section at the annual meeting of the British Association for the Advancement of Science, Glasgow, September

Raffe, D., Howieson, C., and T. Tinklin, (2007), "The impact of a unified curriculum and qualifications system: the Higher Still reform of post-16 education in Scotland", *British Educational Research Journal*, Vol. 33 (in press).

SE (Scottish Executive) (2003p), *Pupils in Scotland*, Scottish Executive, Edinburgh.

SE (Scottish Executive) (2005s), *Social Focus on Deprived Areas 2005,* Scottish Executive, Edinburgh.

SE (Scottish Executive) (2006g), *Scottish Index of Multiple Deprivation 2006: General report,* Scottish Executive, Edinburgh.

SE (Scottish Executive) (2006m), *Statistics Publication Notice: Economy Series: Scottish Households below average income 2004/05,* Scottish Executive National Statistics, Edinburgh.

SEED (Scottish Executive Education Department) (2004a), *Statistics Publication Notice: Education Series: 5-14 Attainment in Publicly Funded Schools 2003/04 (by June 2004),* Scottish Executive National Statistics, Edinburgh.

SEED (Scottish Executive Education Department) (2005q), *Statistics Publication Notice: Education Series: SQA Attainment and School Leaver Qualifications in Scotland: 2003/04,* Scottish Executive National Statistics, Edinburgh.

SEED (Scottish Executive Education Department) (2006s), *Scottish Survey of Achievement: Information: 2005 Scottish Survey of Achievement (SSA) English Language and Core Skills,* Scottish Executive, Edinburgh.

SEED (Scottish Executive Education Department) (2007i), *Statistics Publication Notice: Education Series: SQA Attainment and School Leaver Qualifications in Scotland: 2005/06,* Scottish Executive National Statistics, Edinburgh.

SQA (Scottish Qualifications Authority) (2006q), "Scottish Qualifications", *http://www.scqf.org.uk/table.htm*

Teese, R. and J. Polesel (2003), *Undemocratic Schooling. Equity and Quality in Mass Secondary Education in Australia,* Melbourne University Press, Melbourne.

5. *Staying on at School, Building on School*

In this chapter, the OECD review team discusses the participation of young people in post-compulsory education and training and the destinations of school leavers more broadly. There are two main concerns in this chapter. Firstly, are young people who are successful in school building on their success through different forms of post-compulsory education and training (not necessarily school)? Secondly, do young people who are less successful have good opportunities for further study and training so that they can reverse the economic and cultural effects of under-achievement at school?

Before considering these questions in detail, it is important to establish the context. There are four parts to this: (1) changes in the industry and occupational structure of the Scottish economy, and in labour markets; (2) cultural changes in expectations about achievement at school and in aspirations for careers; (3) the capacity of different sections of the Scottish population to manage economic and social change; and (4) changes in the extent to which young people use formal education and in the balance of activity across sectors of education and training.

Economic change

Figure 5.1 shows employment trends by industry sector over the decade 1996-2006. The most pronounced trends are the fall in manufacturing employment—a loss of nearly every third job—and the growth in services. Public sector employment added 164 000 jobs to more than offset the loss of 128 000 jobs in manufacturing. Banking, finance and insurance added a further 95 000 jobs over this period.

It is projected that there will be further strong growth in business services over the next decade to 2017, continuing growth in health and social work (and to a lesser extent education), and further falls in manufacturing, engineering, food, drink and tobacco processing and agriculture and fishery (Futureskills Scotland, 2007, p. 22).

Figure 5.1 Employment change by industry sector, 1996-2006 ('000s)

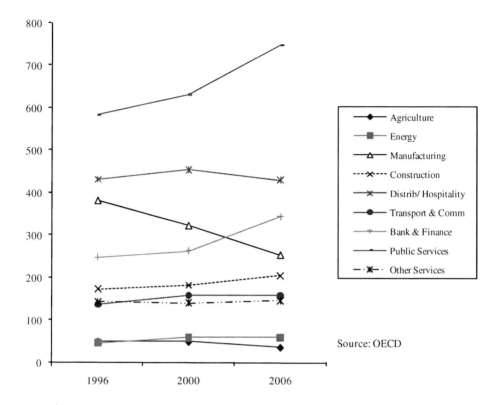

Source: OECD

Changes in the industry structure of the Scottish economy are driving changes in the pattern of occupations. For example, employment in skilled trades has fallen from around 350 000 jobs in 1987 to about 330 000 in 2007 and is expected to fall more sharply over the next decade. There have also been heavy falls in low-skill manual work, and substantial falls in jobs for process workers and plant and machine operators. By contrast, strong growth has occurred in jobs for managers and senior officials, professionals, and technicians and associate professionals. These occupational areas are very large sources of employment in Scotland, not only sources of growth. Figure 5.2, from Futureskills Scotland, reports occupational trends.

Figure 5.2 Projected changes in occupations, 1987-2017 (000s)

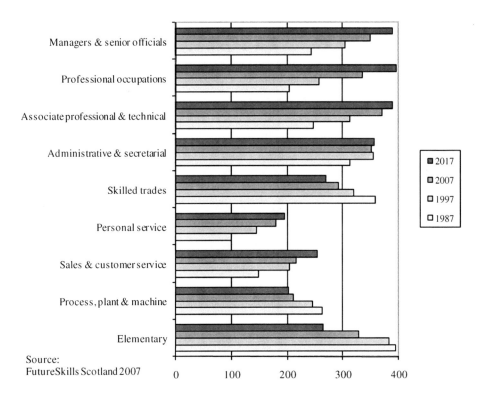

Source:
FutureSkills Scotland 2007

The expansion of the services economy places increasing pressure on the Scottish workforce to reskill and to obtain higher qualifications. Otherwise workers risk being trapped in declining industries, performing jobs in less and less demand. Even in industries, such as construction, which have traditionally been dominated by skilled trades, employment growth in the decade to 2006 has favoured people with upper secondary education and tertiary qualifications. More apprenticeships are now going to young people with upper secondary qualifications, as was pointed out to the OECD review team by Scottish teachers. However, in the growth industries of the economy, such as human services, and banking, finance and insurance, this is still more pronounced. Figure 5.3 shows growth in employment by industry sector and by level of qualification between 1996 and 2006.

Figure 5.3 Employment trend by sector and education level, 1996-2006

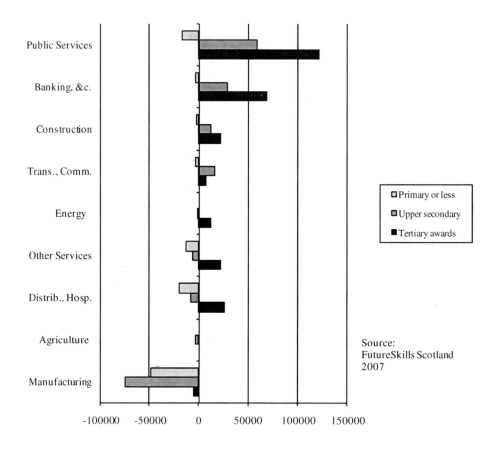

These broad changes in industry and occupational structure are taking place throughout the United Kingdom, in western Europe and in other OECD countries. However, the labour market impact of the changes varies within the OECD. In some countries, employment growth has occurred across the range of jobs, including those held by poorly educated workers. This is the case, for example, in the UK taken as a whole, the United States, the Netherlands, Spain and New Zealand. However, in other countries, there has been a marked fall in jobs held by workers with low levels of education. For example, in Germany and Austria, these jobs have been in decline, while aggregate employment has risen. This is also the case in Belgium, Denmark, Greece and Italy. It is also the case with Scotland. Jobs held by workers with limited education are shrinking (see Figure 5.4).

Figure 5.4 Annual average growth in total employment and in jobs held by low-educated workers, 1993-2002 (%)

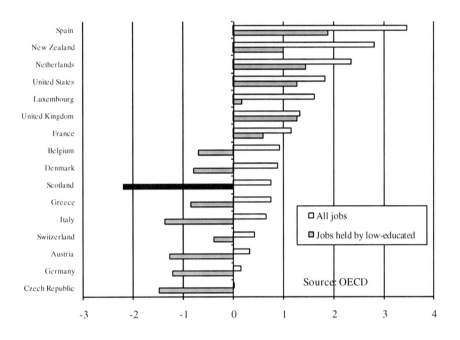

Workers who have not completed secondary school and have undertaken no further formal education or training since leaving school are at particular risk of unemployment. This is true in many OECD countries. In Scotland, the gap in unemployment between the highest and the lowest qualified workers is at the higher end for its comparator OECD nations. Only 3 in 100 of the most well-qualified workers were unemployed in 2006 compared to 11.4% of the least qualified (Figure 5.5).

While the impact of labour market change in Scotland on poorly educated workers and their families is high, its intensity varies from region to region and from city to city, depending on local industry patterns. Edinburgh, a large proportion of whose workforce is employed in public and business services, had one of the lowest unemployment rates amongst European cities in 2001 (3.8%). Glasgow, on the other hand, with a different industry structure and history, had amongst the highest (11.3%). This makes the performance of schools and opportunities for further study and training of critical importance in breaking the poverty cycle.

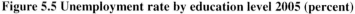

Figure 5.5 Unemployment rate by education level 2005 (percent)

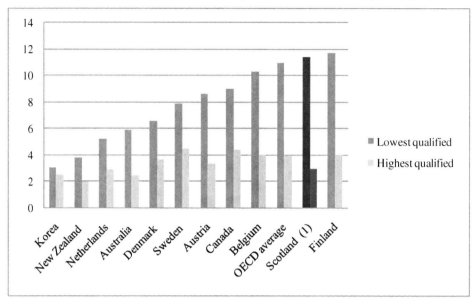

Source: OECD Education Statistics

(1) Data for 2006; Source: Scottish Government

Cultural change

The context in which staying on at school and post-school transition are judged is not only economic, but cultural. The clearest manifestation of this is the way in which expectations begin to shift regarding the kind of person education systems should prepare and the kinds of knowledge they should transmit. Through *A Curriculum for Excellence*, Scotland offers a very clear picture of the ideal towards which it is seeking to orient, not only its schools, but the whole of its educational effort. The purpose is to enable all young people to become successful learners, confident individuals, responsible citizens, and effective contributors.

Such pictures have been composed in the past. But always behind them has been a class assumption. They were portraits of an aristocracy or of the rising middle classes. In Scotland, there has been a long tradition of popular education, involving a much more open view of who might be educated and also of what counts as a good or at any rate useful education. But economic conditions have generally checked the democratic impulse and consequently also have narrowed intellectual horizons.

The major changes that have occurred in the Scottish economy over the last three decades have created an environment in which higher, more effective and more rounded schooling for all is seen as necessary and within reach, and in which the intellectual horizons of good schooling have again broadened. We might seek a parallel in the late seventeenth-century, with the teaching of science, commerce, modern languages, and geography to a widening social group, when Scotland was a leader, on the edge of economic expansion. But we only have to consider the profound transformation of the Scottish workforce in recent decades in terms both of occupations and qualifications to see that cultural demands would almost certainly follow and that schools would be asked to achieve much more in the intellectual depth and the social breadth of their work.

Young people themselves recognize the directions of economic growth and pitch their aspirations accordingly. Survey findings from PISA indicate that nearly three in four students aged 15 expect to be employed by age 30 in high-skilled, white collar occupations. This exceeds the likely capacity of the Scottish economy. But it also reflects how the dominant sector, both of current employment and growth, sets the scene. This is not unconnected with how the changing world is interpreted by schools. A strong emphasis on examinations in subjects of an academic or general kind favours 'middle class' aspirations and offers a practical induction into white collar work. In contrast to this, only about 10% of PISA respondents expect to be doing skilled manual work by age 30. This is roughly in line with the current share of skilled trades in the Scottish economy—in 2007, they contributed 11% of all jobs (Futureskills Scotland, 2007, p. 29).

Rising occupational aspirations require greater educational effort, including extended schooling, success at school (not just participation), and entry to college or university. Around 60% of respondents in the 2003 Scottish Survey School Leavers (SSLS) said that they wanted to go to university and get a degree (Anderson *et al.*, 2004, p. 65). It is notable that this is a broadly-based aspiration in social terms. For over 40% of young people from the poorest family backgrounds want to go to university (Anderson *et al.*, 2004, p. 67). While this is less than half the level of aspiration amongst young people from higher professional and managerial backgrounds, it reveals both a responsiveness to economic change—a willingness to adapt—and greater uncertainty and insecurity in the face of change. For lower aspirations amongst poorer families are a reflection of the much greater risks of academic failure that confront them in school and the much greater economic pressure under which they are placed through debt, earnings foregone, and higher education costs. Economic change threatens these families more than others. How well they respond depends greatly on what schools have to offer and how well they work.

How Scotland's people are placed to respond to economic change

Most of the growth in employment that will occur in Scotland over the next decade will be to replace retiring workers. A small proportion of total growth will be due to economic expansion. Replacement occurs through a set of different processes. These include the re-skilling of the employed population, greater participation in the workforce by people not previously active, reductions in unemployment and underemployment, and immigration. However, the primary source of replacement is demographic renewal through young entrants to the workforce. Renewal has to be adequate in both quantitative and qualitative terms. To meet emerging labour demand, the education and training system—including enterprise-based training—has to enable people to adjust their efforts so as to exploit emerging opportunities and avoid dead-ends. Given the directions of economic change, the Scottish people need to adjust their efforts upwards so that they are both more qualified and more flexible.

Currently about 12% of the working-age population has no qualifications. They have minimum schooling and no recognized post-school education or training. In the main, these are older people. But every year some 4% of all school leavers quit school without any qualifications. In other words, there is a continual replenishment of the pool of unqualified people of working age at a time of change when the Scottish economy is not able to absorb some of them.

A somewhat larger proportion of the population has qualifications equivalent to Scottish Vocational Qualifications (SVQ) Level 1. This includes young people leaving school with General Standard Grades (Futureskills Scotland, 2007, p. 16). The labour market can absorb most of these exit students, through the many part-time, casual, low-skill and low-paid jobs that have been created in the retail, food and hospitality sectors. As much as 40% of total employment of 16-24 year-olds is accounted for by these sectors.[4]

As the workforce of Scotland is renewed over the next decade, it is projected that there will be a major fall in the number of workers without any qualifications (a loss of over 100 000 jobs). This represents about 44%

---

[4]   Secretariat estimates based on the European Union Labour Force Survey for the EU countries; Scottish Executive for Scotland; OECD database on services for the other countries.

or nearly every second job held by an unqualified worker (Futureskills Scotland, 2007, p. 18). There will be a much smaller fall in employment amongst the larger group of workers holding minimal qualifications (a loss of 65 000 jobs or 17% of all jobs held by this group).

For school leavers, these trends imply that basically there will be no work for those without qualifications. They will have to compete for far fewer jobs against older workers, including young people marginally better educated than them. If they are successful, they will have the poorest paid jobs and occupy the most precarious positions in the labour market. The young people with minimal qualifications will also be competing over a declining number of jobs, and the most intense competition will come from their better-qualified peers. There will be fewer and fewer apprenticeships— following a now well-established trend—and employers will tend to choose older, more mature and more mobile teenagers or young adults.

It is within the context of these trends that current patterns in staying-on at school and post-school transition have to be considered. If the pool of jobs for unqualified workers is drying up, there will be heavy costs to pay for a continued outflow of school leavers who have not gained even minimal qualifications—costs both individual and social. While the pool of jobs for minimally-qualified workers will contract only half as much (in relative terms), this too will sharply narrow opportunities for school leavers with only average Standard Grades. They will face wider and more diverse competition, and, if they fail, they also will pay heavy costs in the form of ongoing precariousness.

The use of formal education and the balance across sectors

Since the Second World War, the populations of developed countries— but not only these—have become increasingly dependent in an economic sense on formal education. This is most clearly evident in the rising use of school. In the later decades of the post-war period, the decline of manufacturing industry and the growth of the services sector have increased economic dependence, not only on school, but on further and higher education as well. Older and less educated individuals have become more vulnerable as traditional sources of employment have been exhausted, and younger people have had to extend their use of school to access new sources of employment.

Scotland, as we have seen, is no exception to this general pattern. The qualification levels of the population are rising—and are expected to rise still further in search of the jobs which the Scottish economy is creating. But whether this expectation of overall performance will be fulfilled, and whether all sections of the population are able to access emerging economic opportunities will depend on the inclusiveness and the flexibility of the education system.

The OECD review has a particular interest in schools, but also the points of transition with other sectors of education and training, including non-formal and on-the-job training. How well young people use school greatly influences their subsequent pattern of educational activity, including the sectors in which this occurs, the qualification levels at which this does occur, and whether or not they complete their studies or training. The quality of young people's achievement at school is thus paramount. This puts the performance of Scottish schools into a particular perspective. It is thanks to them that a more or less strong platform of individual achievement is created. Each post-school sector will add value to what schools have done, and be able to play distinctive and specialist roles, reflecting their comparative advantage in training markets. At the very least, they will compensate for what schools have failed to do or should have done better, while at their best, they will do things that schools cannot do. Is this the way that post-compulsory education and training work in Scotland? Let us begin with the platform-building role of schools.

The use of school

It should be stressed from the outset that standards of attainment in Scottish schools have been rising. The significance of this trend should not be overlooked. For it means that the potential to 'add value' through more specific, applied or intensive education and training is growing.

The improving standard of schools is borne out by National Survey results, *e.g.*, the falls that have occurred in the proportions of S2 pupils under-achieving in mathematics. Another sign is the trend to higher levels of attainment in Standard Grades. In the mid-nineties, only 10% of all school leavers achieved at high levels (Levels 1 or 2). This rose steadily to represent about 28% in 2004/05 (The Poverty Site, 2007) (see Figure 5.6).

Findings from the Scottish Survey of School Leavers (SSLS) also point to a continuing upward trend in attainment. To quote from the 2003 report, "This is most marked at the highest level of attainment with a significant increase in [students] obtaining 5 or more passes at 1-3/A-C [levels], an increase of 9 per cent." (Anderson *et al.*, 2004, p. 69). In other words, better students are getting better—a trend noted by HMIe (2006m). An analysis by Croxford and Raffe (2005) shows that between 1984 and 1999, the average attainment score of 16 year-olds in Scotland nearly doubled.

Figure 5.6 School leavers and highest qualifications, 1997 to 2005

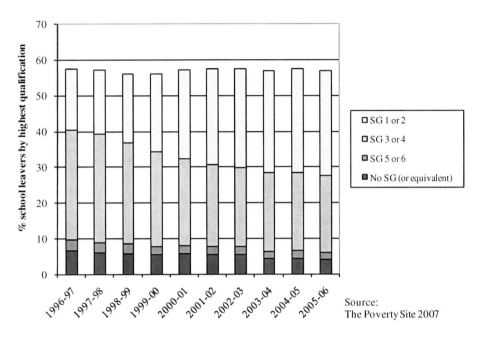

Source:
The Poverty Site 2007

These indicators of an improving standard in school achievement mean that the platform is being raised for more successful use of school at post-compulsory levels and also for greater use of college opportunities. It does not necessarily follow that more of an age-cohort will enrol in university. But rising achievement in compulsory school does open up this possibility—along with the rising aspirations that might be expected to accompany it.

On the evidence available, however, it is not clear that improved achievement in the compulsory years **is** carrying forward into more successful participation in the post-compulsory years of school. Firstly, there has been very little change over the last seven years in the proportion of a cohort entering S5. Figure 5.7 shows that around 71% of girls and 63% of boys stay on to S5, and that there has been little trend in these figures over the period 1999-2005. Similarly, there has been practically no change in the proportions of S3 pupils staying on to S6 (Breitenbach and Wasoff, 2007),

Each year, about 1 in 3 young people end school when their legal obligation is complete. This does not mean that they end their involvement in education and training. Rather it means that they end their connection with **school**, and also that this is a persistent pattern.

Figure 5.7 Staying on rates in Scotland, 1996-2005 (%)

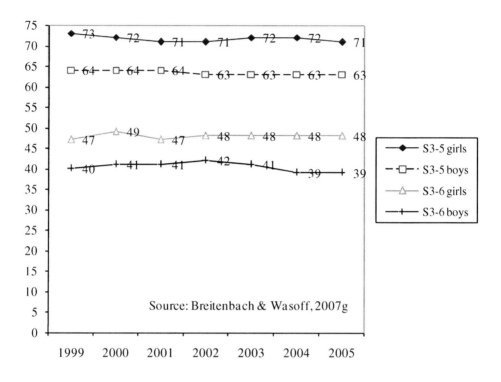

Source: Breitenbach & Wasoff, 2007g

The second indication that improving achievement in the compulsory years does not appear to be leading to more successful participation in the post-compulsory years of school is a qualitative one. Analysis of pass rates in national qualifications examinations by prior level of attainment in Standard Grades shows that there are continuing very large gaps (Raffe, Howieson and Tinklin, 2007). This is true even though the opportunity structure has been broadened and made more flexible. Is there any evidence that, in the most recent years, this pattern has changed?

Stability in staying-on rates and persistence in attainment gaps suggest that while Scottish schools succeed in taking two-thirds of a cohort into the post-compulsory years, they are not 'converting' higher levels of attainment into more and better participation in school during these years.

It appears, then, that the rising platform of attainment in compulsory school is supporting already-successful students to stay on at school, but not expanding the use of school to less successful students. Support for better students extends to improving their competitive advantage by increasing their capacity to undertake more challenging work, *e.g.*, Advanced Highers. Less successful students, on the other hand, have not lifted their participation in upper secondary school, despite increased flexibility in the curriculum. Their staying-on rates are lower and, if they do stay on, their performance is poorer. As we shall see, they use other pathways to build on the more limited degree of success they have achieved.

The qualification levels of school leavers

The rift between high and low achievers in school continuation rates and in pass rates in upper secondary education is not only an academic, but a social divide. Young people from the poorest family backgrounds are nearly four times more likely than students not in poverty to quit school without any qualifications at all (11% compared to less than 3%). Despite the complexity of qualifications in Scotland, the impact of poverty on 'who gets what' is unmistakable (see Figure 4.12 in Chapter 4 contains a comparison from SE, 2005q).

Figure 5.8 Attainment of Standard Grades (number and level)
by socio-economic status (%)

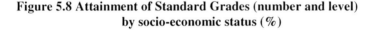

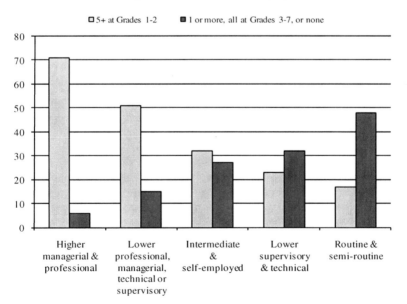

Source: Anderson, Biggart, Deakin *et al.* 2004

To guard against the view that deprivation is the sole or main factor behind unequal attainment, it is helpful to note the analysis of Standard Grades by socio-economic status available from the SSLS. Findings from the 2003 survey show that while 71% of school leavers from upper managerial and professional backgrounds achieved at least five grades at 1-2 Level, this fell away consistently to reach a low of only 17% amongst school leavers from semi-skilled and unskilled manual workers' homes (Anderson *et al.*, 2004, p. 70) (Figure 5.8). Conversely, only 6% of the socially most advantaged group attained very low qualifications (or none) as compared to 48% amongst the least advantaged school leavers. As the SSLS report concludes, there is a "strong linear relationship with attainment as we move up or down the social class hierarchy".

From school to further study or training

Staying-on rates in school are not a good guide to the extent to which young people in Scotland build on schooling. There are other ways in which investment in further study or training occurs. Since 1993, there has been a steady increase in transition to further education colleges, rising from 15% to 23% (Careers Scotland, 2007u). The significance of this trend lies partly in the ability of the colleges to help young people make the transition to the growing services sector of the Scottish economy. This is in the context of declining opportunities in manufacturing industry, especially apprenticeships. Figure 5.9 reports the divergent trends in school leaver destinations since the early 1990s.

Colleges are able to play this 'brokerage' role thanks to a strong interface with business and industry, flexibility in programmes, and a social intake that is much wider than that of higher education institutions, especially the older ones.

The upward trend in school-to-college transition is also important because it involves a widening access to higher education. It is estimated that in 2000/02, further education colleges accounted for over a third of all undergraduate students in Scottish higher education (Gallacher and MacFarlane, 2003, p. 2). The importance of this level of provision lies in the more vocationally oriented and flexible nature of the higher national qualifications (HNQs) delivered by the colleges as well as greater social equity. HNQs, in turn, also provide a route to universities (mainly the post-1992 institutions). About 13 in 100 commencing undergraduates in Scottish universities hold a higher national qualification as their highest award (Gallacher and MacFarlane, 2003, p. 17).

Figure 5.9 Destinations of Scottish school leavers by education and training sectors -- variations from average levels since 1992/93 (%)

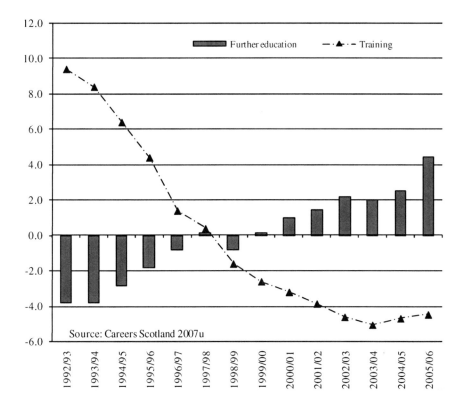

Source: Careers Scotland 2007u

Since the early 1990s, more and more school leavers have enrolled in higher education. However, this trend peaked in 2000/01 and has since fallen back to the levels of the late 1990s. The age participation index of higher education for young Scots stood at 47.1% in 2005/06. Change in Scottish participation (covering both universities and FE colleges) is presented in Figure 5.10. This represents a comparatively high level of access to higher education by OECD standards. In 2003, the country average for access to type A tertiary education was 53%. For the United Kingdom as a whole, it was 48% (OECD, 2004, Table C2.2). The comparable Scottish figure was 57% (SG, 2007c).

Figure 5.10 Age-participation index of higher education in Scotland, 1984-2006 (%)

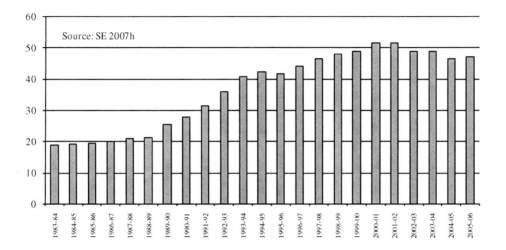

Figure 5.11 Study and training destinations of school leavers, 1993-2006

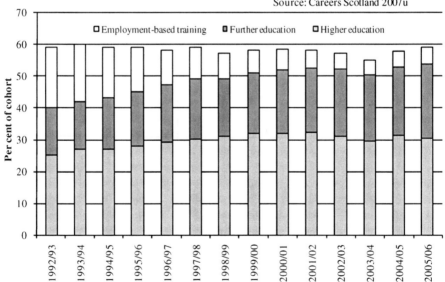

The upward trend in further education enrolments and the comparatively high level of enrolment in higher education suggest that marked inequalities in school attainment have not prevented a majority of young Scots from investing in further study. However, total transition to **further education and training** has been static for over a decade. This has been due to two factors: (1) the sharp downturn in apprenticeships undertaken by school leavers, and (2) fairly limited growth in higher education, which peaked in 2000/01. It is the colleges that have contributed most of the overall improvement in study activity. These trends are reported in Figure 5.11 (Careers Scotland, 2007u). Employment-based training refers to accredited learning rather than informal on-the-job training.

From school to work

Inequalities in school attainment have affected the **level of study** undertaken by school leavers (vocational/non-advanced vs. higher education) and the **sector and institutions** of study (college vs. university, ancient vs. modern). But poorer success at school is also associated with non-participation in **any** form of post-school study. Low achievers are progressively excluded from formal education and take their chances in the labour market. The further education sector remains open to them, but the early years of transition are a time of precariousness for many school leavers who have not done well at school.

About 13 in 100 young people are unemployed on leaving school. Most are seeking work or training. Those with the most troubled history of schooling (regular truant, expelled or suspended) have a substantially higher risk of unemployment as do young people with multiple disadvantages (Anderson *et al.*, 2004, p. 85).

Many school leavers—just over one in four—do find work. For this group, it is important to consider the level of their employment (part-time vs. full-time), whether it is linked with training (not necessarily formal), and whether there are employee protections and good conditions of work. In this report, we can only touch on the issue of level of employment.

Official tables on school leaver destinations do not distinguish between full- and part-time work. This is a matter of concern. There does not appear to be a consistent view about just how much work Scottish school leavers do have. The SSLS 2003 finding is that only 15% of school leavers whose main activity was work were employed part-time. Part-time is defined as 19 hours per week (Anderson *et al.*, 2004, p. 48). National statistics, on the other hand, classify every fourth worker as part-time (SE, 2006e, Table 4.6). In some occupations, the percentage of part-time workers is higher, *e.g.*, junior non-manual jobs (retail, food, hospitality). At least a third of all people in these occupations have 26 hours per week or less (SE, 2002e, Table 3.15, 2001 data; SE, 2007e, Table 4.6). These are occupations held by very large numbers of young people. With the decline of apprenticeships, it is likely that every fourth school leaver at a minimum has only part-time (and frequently casual) work. This includes those receiving some form of recognized training. However, much greater clarity is needed on this point.

Under-achievement and unemployment

Young people who experience sustained periods of unemployment or can find only part-time work are not a homogeneous group. However, low attainment and low self-esteem frequently contribute to poor transition and continuing difficulties in adjustment and are common factors. Under-achievement casts a long shadow. It pursues young people into the labour market, limiting their acceptance by employers and eroding their confidence in themselves. It gives them access mainly to low-paying, temporary and unsatisfying or unchallenging work, usually uncompensated by training on the job.

While the origins of unemployment do not lie simply in the attributes of individuals, neither is under-achievement simply an attribute of individuals considered in isolation. Because it is more highly concentrated in some geographical areas than others—representing a common experience—it can acquire the force of a cultural fact. Since schooling is the key institutional point at which the transmission of social disadvantage has the most chance of being broken, persistent high levels of under-achievement have a depressing effect on communities and undermine confidence in the power of school, but also of individuals themselves. This contributes to creating a culture of despair which is antithetical to employment and enterprise and which feeds on other sources of disillusionment, such as poor public safety, crime, poor housing, and lack of amenities.

Without seeking to attribute causality, there is a strong social area association in Scotland between under-achievement at school and unemployment levels amongst school leavers. The connection between the two is no doubt more complex than poor qualifications and lack of labour market competitiveness. But it is important to highlight these two factors and recognize the cultural interactions between them. Figure 5.12 shows that the higher the proportion of pupils under-achieving in S2, the higher the proportion of young people who are unemployed on leaving school (derived from SE, 2004a and SE, 2006d).

Figure 5.12 Under-achievement and unemployment by local authority

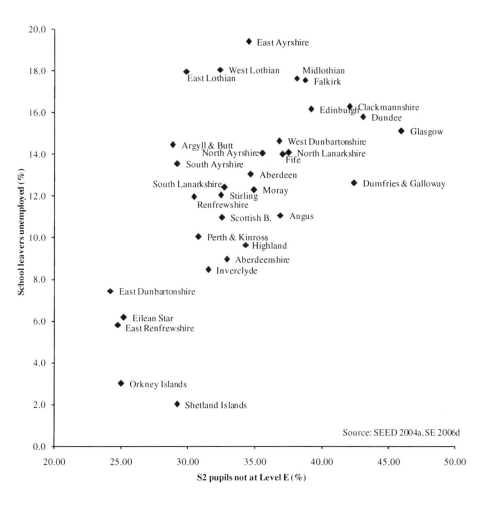

The association between under-achievement and unemployment makes the point that government needs to address two clearly distinct, but related phenomena. It cannot advance on one front without advancing on the other, as is recognized in *More Choices, More Chances* (SE, 2006n).

NEET—not in education, employment or training

We have stressed the issue of under-achievement in our discussion of transition from school to work because it underlies a major national concern in Scotland—the comparatively high proportion of young people who are not in education, employment or training (NEET). It is estimated that there are a total of 35 000 young people in this category (or 13.5% of the age group 16-19), of whom 20 000 (or 7.7%) are defined as needing additional support (SE, 2006n, p. 1). The composition of the group is also diverse. As many as 40% are inactive through sickness, disability or caring responsibilities (SE, 2006n, p. 5).

NEET is a statistical category which captures a range of different individuals in the course of their education, employment and social trajectories. Almost half of this group (44%) shift into employment or education, while just over half (56%) remain in a precarious situation, either unemployed or inactive. The incidence of NEET is greater in certain local authorities in Scotland—Glasgow (19.1%), Clackmannanshire (16.9%), Dundee (14.2%), East Ayrshire (16.4%), North Ayrshire (17.4%), Inverclyde (15.1), and West Dunbartonshire (15.9%). As *More Choices, More Chances* notes, this is a "clear indication of a significant structural problem in the local area" (SE, 2006n p. 10).

Scotland has an overarching strategy to tackle poor transition and precariousness. It involves prevention (pre-16); youth services support with an emphasis on education and training for long-term employability (post-16); financial incentives for re-engaging in education; 'key workers' support or case-management to deliver services; and partnerships at national and local levels to co-ordinate action, including through a national NEET Delivery Team.

Within this strategy, prevention of poor transitions through a more satisfactory experience of school has a strong emphasis. Young people classified as NEET represent 20% of all school leavers in Scotland (SE, 2006n, Table 2, p. 46). This suggests a lot of uncertainty in the early phase of transition from school. However, in some regions the proportion is much higher—every fourth school leaver in Aberdeen City, Clackmannanshire, Falkirk, North Lanarkshire, and South Ayrshire; and as many as 30% in Glasgow City.

Schools have developed more vocational options and links with local business and industry to improve student engagement and achievement. But the picture in 2005 has been described as a "mixed model of patchy provision which limits the options that can be offered to young people" (SE, 2006n, §48, p. 16).

The high rates of "negative school leaver destinations" (SE, 2006n, p. 47) observed in some of the largest local authorities in Scotland should be viewed in the context of the apparent lack of growth in school staying-on rates, the long-term decline in employment-based training, and the limited (though important) growth in further education destinations.

Figure 5.13 Percentages of 15-19 year-olds in education or training, 2003

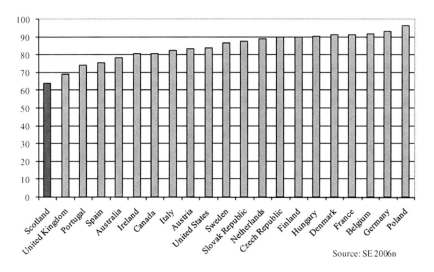

Source: SE 2006n

These trends underlie Scotland's comparatively poor position in terms of the proportion of 15-19 year-olds in education. Figure 5.13, reproduced from the national NEET strategy publication (SE, 2006n, p. 53), shows that Scotland has a fairly low profile of educational participation, in part because of high participation rates in the workforce (though not necessarily in the employed workforce).

The institutional framework of post-compulsory education and training does not seem to be responding adequately to the economic pressures on young people to invest more in further study and training, or to be responding equitably to the impact of these pressures on the most academically and economically vulnerable groups of young people.

While a preventative (pre-16) action plan is in place, the key components of this plan that relate to curriculum are broadly formulated, lack clear institutional accountability, and fall short of a nationally defined programme of studies. It is left to schools and local authorities to implement a *Curriculum for Excellence* and Assessment is for Learning and to provide more varied opportunities for student success, including vocational options, partnerships with business, and links with colleges. It is envisaged that the structure of qualifications will be simplified to improve progression by reviewing Standard Grade and its links with other national qualifications. However, manipulating the qualifications structure is not a substitute for developing nationally-accessible programmes of applied learning or for renovating existing courses in light of their transition effectiveness and pedagogical inclusiveness. It appears that too much reliance is being placed on diffuse measures of improvement, especially at the school level, and too little effort is being applied to rethinking curriculum in terms of economic incentives and economic impact for all young people. In Scotland, high achievers enjoy the greatest certainty of transition, resting on the clearest programme pathways that enjoy national endorsement and acceptance. The weakest achievers experience the greatest uncertainty and have the poorest defined programme pathways, whose flexibility is viewed as a strength, not a necessity.

Conclusion

This chapter has been concerned with two basic issues. Do young people in Scotland build on successful schooling through continued education or training, including upper secondary education, and do young people who have been less successful at school have good opportunities to reverse the effects of under-achievement and make an effective transition into working life?

We raised these questions in the context of major long-term changes in the industry and occupational structure of the Scottish economy—changes that will require higher levels of achievement from all young people. The transformation of Scotland's economy is echoed in both official thinking on curriculum and standards, and in the aspirations of young people themselves.

Turning to patterns of educational participation, we noted first of all that there has been an improving standard in Scottish education. Achievement, as measured in a number of ways, has been rising. This means a stronger platform for young people's aspirations and for continued investment in education and training beyond the compulsory years. However, we observed (a) little change in staying-on rates at school, (b) very little recent change in transition to higher education, and (c) continuing growth in further education.

It appears that limits have been reached in the growth of upper secondary education. Either the one in three young people who leave school at age 16 do not see sufficient incentive to continue or schools lack the programmes or the teaching strengths to accommodate them. Instead, expansion is occurring through the further education sector. The colleges offer a different environment, greater flexibility in their programmes, linkages with employment, accessible courses in higher education, and the possibility also of entering university with credit transfer. Schools themselves have contributed to this pattern by offering vocational options through the colleges.

If schools have reached their limit, does it really matter that colleges have taken the relay? Surely they are best suited through their programmes, facilities, and specialist staff to manage the particular needs of young people leaving at the end of compulsory school? There are mixed views about this in Scotland. Here we would like to sound a note of caution. How will schools learn to manage diversity if they export the challenge to colleges? There is a risk that by not developing strong vocational programmes, schools will entrench their academic culture and continually reproduce the gaps in achievement which mark compulsory secondary education and the "dip" in overall performance that is commonly observed. If weaker learners are destined to become someone else's responsibility, schools undermine their own enrolment base and starve the senior years of viable numbers. But above all they add to the equity problem. For weaker learners are not a socially random sample of the population.

The issue is not the suitability, effectiveness or prestige of the colleges. Rather it is the potential blunting of the action of schools, the weakening of their role **in the compulsory years**, that may occur through a **selective** use of the colleges to solve the diversity challenge. Were schools to make more expansive use of their college links to benefit *all* categories of students, the issue would not be so critical. In short, schools' commitment to weaker learners is going to be limited when there is a well-established mechanism to relieve them of the need.

Failure to manage diversity more effectively over the four years of compulsory secondary education means a continued problem of poor transition, but also a continual narrowing of the social base of the upper stages of secondary education. Colleges play a major role in compensating for this as they make higher education available to many young people. But many young people also want the chance to study at university, and the directions of economic change increasingly require them to do so.

References

Anderson, S *et al.* (2004), 17 in 2003 - Findings from the Scottish School Leavers Survey SEED, Edinburgh.

Breitenbach, E. and Wasoff, F. (2007g), *A Gender Audit of Statistics: Comparing the Position of Women and Men in Scotland*, Scottish Executive Social Research, Edinburgh.

Careers Scotland (2007u), Unpublished tables on school leaver transitions.

Croxford, L. and D. Raffe (2005), "Secondary school organisation in England, Scotland and Wales since the 1980s", Paper for the seminar on Policy Learning in 14-19 Education, Joint Seminar of education and youth transitions Project and Nuffield review of 14 – 19 Education, 15 March 2005.

Futureskills Scotland (2007), *"Labour Market Projections 2007 to 2017"*, Scottish Enterprise, Glasgow.

Gallacher, J. and MacFarlane, K. (2003), *Higher national qualifications and higher education in further education colleges*, Scottish Qualifications Authority, Glasgow.

HMIe (2005), *Working Together: Cross Sectoral Provision of Vocational Education*, Her Majesty's Inspectorate of Education, Livingston

HMIe (2006m), *Missing Out: A report on children at risk of missing out on educational opportunities*, Her Majesty's Inspectorate of Education, Livingston.

OECD (2004), *Education at a Glance: OECD Indicators 2004*, Organisation for Economic Co-operation and Development, Paris.

Raffe, D., Howieson, C., and T. Tinklin, (2007), "The impact of a unified curriculum and qualifications system: the Higher Still reform of post-16 education in Scotland", *British Educational Research Journal*, Vol. 33 (in press).

SE (Scottish Executive) (2002e), *Scotland's People*, Volume 5, tables on hours worked, Scottish Executive Publications, Edinburgh.

SE (Scottish Executive) (2006d), *Destinations of leavers from Scottish schools: 2005/06*, Scottish Executive National Statistics, Edinburgh.

SE (Scottish Executive) (2006e), *Scottish Economic Statistics 2006*, Scottish Executive, Edinburgh.

SE (Scottish Executive) (2006n), *More Choices, More Chances: A Strategy to Reduce the Proportion of Young People not in Education, Employment or Training in Scotland*, Scottish Executive, Edinburgh, http://www.scotland.gov.uk/Resource/Doc/129456/0030812.pdf

SE (Scottish Executive) (2007e), *Scottish Economic Statistics 2007*, Scottish Executive, Edinburgh.

SE (Scottish Executive) (2007h), *Statistics Publication Notice: Lifelong Learning Series: The Age Participation Index for Scotland 2005 -06*, Scottish Executive National Statistics, Edinburgh.

SEED (Scottish Executive Education Department) (2004a), *Statistics Publication Notice: Education Series: 5-14 Attainment in Publicly Funded Schools 2003/04 (by June 2004)*, Scottish Executive National Statistics, Edinburgh.

SEED (Scottish Executive Education Department) (2005q), *Statistics Publication Notice: Education Series: SQA Attainment and School Leaver Qualifications in Scotland: 2003/04*, Scottish Executive National Statistics, Edinburgh.

SG (Scottish Government) (2007c). Students in Higher Education--Higher Education Students in Scotland, *http://www.scotland.gov.uk/Topics/Statistics/Browse/Lifelong-learning/TrendHEStudents*

The Poverty Site website (2007), "Educational attainment at age 11", *http://www.poverty.org.uk/S14/index.shtml*

6. *Reforming the Curriculum*

Scotland presents a paradox. It performs at a very high level on PISA tests—both in overall standard and in equity. But viewed from the inside—in terms of national tests and qualifications—it is marked by inequalities. How can the country go forward to achieve much greater consistency in student achievement, while at the same time not diminishing its competitiveness as reflected in PISA rankings?

Scotland's approach to this challenge is multi-sided. It includes the Teachers' Agreement, major investment in infrastructure, high quality teacher induction and headship training programmes, an independent inspection, and whole-of-government approaches to deprivation. But while all of these initiatives aim at improving conditions in schools and the effectiveness of teaching and leadership, their success ultimately depends on the quality of the demands made on children themselves.

Curriculum is the vehicle through which a consistently high level of student achievement is pursued. The existing 5-14 curriculum is today seen as reflecting a stage in educational growth which has now been exceeded. The statutory leaving age is 16, not 14, and most young people stay on for at least one year more. The curriculum that was designed to dramatically widen participation in school has succeeded. But is it the curriculum to build further on the much higher aspirations and fuller experience of school of Scotland's people?

Our concern in this chapter is with Scotland's current efforts to reform the curriculum. We see this in the context of the challenge to resolve major inequalities in student achievement and transition, while maintaining the high overall standards that will enable Scottish children to play a valuable role in tackling the global challenges of the twenty-first century.

A Curriculum for Excellence

Scotland has embarked on a major programme of curriculum reform. This began with the National Debate in 2002. Participants valued the comprehensive principle of Scottish education, the breadth and depth of the

5-14 curriculum, the quality of teaching and of teaching support materials, and also the flexibility of the curriculum. There was no support for a more prescriptive system. On the other hand, participants felt that the curriculum was over-crowded, that there could be better connections across the 3-18 stages, that there needed to be a better balance between "academic" and "vocational" studies, and that assessment and certification should be supporting, not driving student learning. Significantly the debate highlighted the importance of incentives for learning—both intrinsic and extrinsic. There should be greater enjoyment in schoolwork, more attention to skills for tomorrow's workforce, and greater student choice.

In November 2003, a Curriculum Review Group was established to consider the purposes of a new 3-18 curriculum and the principles of design that should govern the creation of that curriculum. The work of this group is reported in *A Curriculum For Excellence* (SEED, 2004c).

A Curriculum for Excellence proceeds from a values standpoint that provides a critical and a continuing frame of reference. From this document, we wish to highlight through somewhat different language the importance of two key features: **incentive-building** in the curriculum through enjoyment, clearly perceived purpose, meaning in schoolwork, and demonstrable value for effort; but also, and through this, **raising achievement**.

The report of the review group has emphasized that the new curriculum should "encourage the development of high levels of accomplishment and intellectual skill" (SEED, 2004c, p. 10). Raising achievement hinges on the extent to which children and young people are successfully engaged in their own learning through intrinsic and extrinsic incentives, respect for different learning styles, and choice in what they study. For older students, high achievement also implies choice in the physical sites and contexts in which learning occurs, including workplaces, community settings and colleges.

Implicitly the double agenda of **incentive building** and **raising achievement** has a social dimension. For at present those learners who enjoy the fewest incentives to work hard at school and whose achievement is also poorest are drawn disproportionately from the poorest or at any rate the least well-educated families in Scotland. So the construction of incentives and the pursuit of higher achievement through the 3-18 curriculum must satisfy a particular test—the quality of learning and the outcomes for students from these families. These students, it cannot be said too often, represent a **large proportion** of all students in Scottish schools. It is the fragile relationship between their families and the schools of Scotland that has to be the particular focus of curriculum reform.

At the same time, the needs of high achievers must not be neglected. An example of the difficulties which they currently face is the sometimes-sharp upswing in academic demand from Standard Grades to Highers. Young people who do manage the existing examinations system well are expected to work effectively across a range of very demanding areas from advanced mathematics to foreign languages. They, too, need the incentives of good teaching, assessment that aids learning, choice in what they study, and economic as well as cultural rewards for the efforts they are asked to make.

A Curriculum for Excellence identifies the formation of "four capacities" as the fundamental purpose of the curriculum. Through school, children should become "successful learners, confident individuals, responsible citizens, and effective contributors". Schools are expected to work towards these goals through the nature of the environments they create—above all, the relationships between people—the range of teaching and learning approaches they encourage, and how cognitive and cultural demands are formed into units of formal learning. Curriculum design is to be guided by a set of principles of variable weight, depending on the stages of schooling. These principles give expression to the concerns raised in the National Debate—challenge and enjoyment, breadth, progression, depth, personalization and choice, coherence and relevance. They could almost be viewed as elements in a charter of rights for children and young people as learners.

The visit of the OECD review team found wide support in schools for the goals and design principles of a *Curriculum for Excellence*. The concerns expressed at the time of the National Debate resounded in schools, and there was keen interest to be involved and to implement the reform agenda. Many schools have registered their interest in contributing to the development and implementation process, drawing on their experience of running programmes which reflect the emphases in the concept papers of the new curriculum. There is clearly an energy for change, and the developmental work of the review group has successfully articulated this. However, the reform process is now in its fifth year—a long interval by comparison with the three major reforms undertaken in Finland in 1985, 1994, and 2004 (Aho, Pitkänen and Sahlberg, 2006). There is a risk of losing momentum along with the enthusiasm and commitment of Scottish educators.

While the purposes, values and design principles have been ably expressed and communicated, detailed development and implementation of the new 3-18 curriculum should involve a more deliberate and focussed engagement with the context of Scottish curriculum reform. This context can be described in terms of (a) the challenges to curriculum and teaching represented by the pattern of student learning and post-school transition outcomes, and (b) the emphasis and the legacy of reform efforts in the recent educational history of Scotland.

The achievement challenge

From our previous chapters, we can summarize the challenges very briefly—the widening achievement gap from about P5; marked social differences in basic achievement in the compulsory years (as reflected in deprivation measures); declining student engagement and interest (especially in early secondary); marked gaps in SQA attainment; staying-on rates that have ceased to grow; wide regional variations in post-compulsory participation (again linked with deprivation); a worrying, comparatively high level of NEET, even using a limited definition; and inequalities in access to higher education.

The new curriculum has been set the task of encouraging the "development of high levels of accomplishment and intellectual skill". As the foundation paper notes, "a significant proportion of young people in Scotland are not achieving all that they are capable of" (SEED, 2004c, p. 10). The challenges identified above will test the 3-18 curriculum, for they are all measures of the distances to be made up through a renewal of Scottish school education, notwithstanding its high overall standing internationally. To address these changes—as well as those arising from the directions of industry and labour market change—will require seeing them in the context of existing institutional arrangements for examinations and qualifications.

The legacy of past curriculum reform

While the National Debate was positive about breadth and depth in the 5-14 curriculum, there were serious concerns about the curriculum in higher stages of schooling. To repeat, issues were raised about connectedness in programmes to age 18, the balance between "academic" and "vocational" studies, and the need for relevant workforce skills, more choice, and an assessment and certification regime which put learning first. These concerns amount to a critique in kinder language of current institutional arrangements that are seen as inflexible, unresponsive, obstructive and outmoded.

During the 1980s, Scotland greatly increased staying-on rates by relaxing access to a largely academic curriculum. The old SCE O grade, to quote the report of the Dunning committee, was "not designed to provide for the substantial group of pupils who are now being presented, but whose abilities permit them to cope only with something less demanding" (SED, 1977, § 1.22). New examinations were introduced, but at different levels of difficulty. This protected children who traditionally made only minimal use of school from a curriculum which was culturally fashioned, both in design and delivery, on the needs of more advantaged children and which barred access through the excessive difficulties it presented. "We are not happy," Dunning complained, "about the narrow aims, inappropriate emphasis and frustrated aspirations which arise in this situation" (SED, 1977, § 1.22).

The reforms of the 1980s were continued at a higher stage of schooling in the 1990s through Higher Still. Adjustments were made to the levels at which courses might be attempted and assessed, thus creating space for low and average achievers to continue on at school.

The legacy of two decades of reform is now crystallized in the institutional arrangements of differentiated course levels, examinations and qualifications. To manage this legacy has required the construction of a complex credit and qualifications framework (the SCQF). For the legacy is a cumulative one, with one layer of examinations being added to another. A major effort has been made to harmonize two different systems of qualifications, without examining the question whether both would still remain necessary. But the bigger question is whether, at least in compulsory school, the approach of differentiating qualification levels is compatible with the objectives of the 3-18 curriculum.

There is no doubt that the Standard Grade reforms accomplished their objective of raising participation by creating manageable space in the curriculum. Children were no longer penalized with failure by having to tackle in compulsory school more than they could reasonably be expected to achieve. But now that the objective of higher participation has been well and truly reached, should the underlying strategy be continued, at least in the compulsory years?

With a national concern for higher achievement, it could be argued that the strategy of syllabus differentiation (to use the language of the Dunning committee) has reached its limits. The curriculum, after all, is meant to challenge and extend, not accommodate and protect. The weaknesses that children present have to be tackled as they are in primary school by good teaching and good programmes, and the weaknesses of teachers in adapting to non-traditional groups have to be tackled by good training, professional development and leadership in schools. Relaxing access to examinations builds confidence and raises aspirations, but at the cost of asking for less and getting less. It is not a long-term strategy.

Varying qualification levels to boost participation is bad for the curriculum itself. It focusses teaching and learning on examinations and puts off indefinitely the need for the contextual and pedagogical adaptation on which all good learning depends. The curriculum becomes a canon, even though it has never been pronounced law. Teachers become administrators of a curriculum that has all the statutory force it needs in examinations. No formal prescription is required when examinations already perform this role.

From lifting participation to raising achievement

In the 1980s, Scotland lowered the examinations platform for weaker learners: today it has to raise the platform of achievement. This is not only for weaker learners. It is to benefit all students through depth and enjoyment of learning. These are the words of *A Curriculum for Excellence*.

Teachers cannot raise the achievement platform except through a curriculum which:

a) offers a breadth of content beyond the most codified forms of knowledge

b) adjusts for differences in cognitive style

c) adjusts for differences in the social context of the school

d) contains demonstrable economic incentives for learning in addition to cultural benefits

e) uses formative and criterion-based assessment

f) is sanctioned by qualifications whose primary purpose is to access pathways to employment, training and further study.

A Curriculum for Excellence offers the broad design principles for major reform in Scotland. But its success will depend on how well it responds to the underlying issues of the achievement gap, uneven student engagement, wide variation in SQA attainment, early leaving and poor transition for some groups, and unequal access to higher education. Will the new curriculum set a course for raising achievement and reducing gaps through breadth of content and approach (**lateral differentiation),** or will it revert to a model of hierarchical and examination-led demands in courses of a largely traditional kind (**vertical differentiation**)? It is too soon to say.

But part of the answer will come from how Scotland approaches the provision of vocational education and training to young people in schools. This is the second major line of curriculum reform and it can be viewed as the single most important avenue for **creating incentives** and for **raising achievement**.

Vocational education and training in curriculum reform

The history of secondary school curriculum reform in OECD countries over the past fifty years has been marked by a number of common trends. These include the modernization of physical and biological sciences curricula, a multi-disciplinary approach to the social sciences, a shift towards more active and less grammar-based methods in modern languages, the development of technology strands, and the teaching of business subjects at senior levels of high school. Many national systems now operate differentiated strands or streams within a school-based curriculum. Vocational education and training has assumed a major role in national curricula. Fields as diverse as food, hospitality, childcare, automotive, construction, electrical, office administration, IT, agriculture and sports have shifted into schools which have become increasingly responsible for workforce training across different industry sectors. They have had to forge relationships with business, industry and community organisations to support this and to develop strategies, such as structured workplace training and school-based apprenticeships, to ensure a high and credible standard of practical training.

These changes have greatly increased participation in upper secondary school at a time when labour market trends have greatly narrowed opportunities for full-time work and employment-based training. In some countries, such as France, much of the growth in participation in the past two decades has been due to the provision of vocational strands at baccalaureat level, while academic programmes have been largely stable.

Economic impacts, such as reducing unemployment, increasing workforce flexibility, meeting skill shortages, and improving earnings have been strongly emphasized in national policy debates. But educators have taken a broader view about the place of VET in schools. Today vocational education and training is seen not only as a strategy of economic adjustment (the prevailing view in the late 1970s and early 1980s), but as a way of lifting educational standards amongst the "non-traditional" populations facing exclusion from the labour market, but struggling for a place in mainly academic high schools.

A balanced strategy should promote vocational education and training to achieve higher achievement standards as well as better employment outcomes, but it should also seek to make the academic curriculum more accessible and inclusive. Without such a strategy, there is a risk that vocational studies will lapse into provision for low achievers from mainly poorer families, while academic studies will languish in routine due to an unchanging social mix of pupils. *A Curriculum for Excellence* does stress the need for change in more academic areas. But what is Scotland's attitude to vocational education and training in schools?

The Scottish view of vocational studies in curriculum reform

The Skills for Work initiative is a very significant development in education policy. For too long, there has been a fear that "vocationalism" will re-introduce the segregated provision of yesteryear. Moreover, there appears to have been a concern that vocational studies are out of step with the directions of economic change. For the services economy calls for higher-order cognitive skills, and for organisational, communication, inter-personal and other generic competencies. This concern—of betraying or short-changing working-class children by relegating them to low-prestige and out-of-date studies—perhaps accounts for the relatively slow and very tentative introduction of vocational options in Scottish secondary schools. It would help explain why Skills for Work courses have been introduced essentially as marginal additions to the mainstream curriculum. As one teacher explained to the OECD review team, "we have been tinkering around the edges".

Behind the fear of a bolder approach to curriculum change is a misconception of the role of vocational studies. The language of the Skills for Work initiative has tended to reinforce this misconception. Employability has been very strongly stressed. This is a major consideration. But it should not be stressed at the expense of the wider educational role of vocational studies. All courses that make up a school curriculum—including vocational courses—should aim at promoting cognitive and personal growth as their first objective. Employability depends on mastery of basic skills, positive attitudes to learning, strong self-esteem, a capacity to work with others, adaptability and responsiveness, and self-directedness. Moreover, the issue is employability **over the long-term** in the context of industry and occupational change—not short-term integration in a labour market which for young people often means only part-time casual work with low pay and little future.

In short, vocational courses should aim, as other courses do, at enduring change in the learner. The difference is that vocational courses contain clearer economic incentives for engagement and also involve alternative approaches to learning. These are the keys to equity. They enable schools to make fuller cognitive and cultural demands on learners—which is the point of the curriculum—as compared to mainstream academic programmes, modelled implicitly on the needs of university-oriented students.

Skills for Work courses have been introduced at the margins of the Scottish curriculum. So there is a risk that the approaches to learning which they involve or encourage may not have an influence over teaching and course design throughout the curriculum. This underlines the importance of implementing vocational courses in the context of a wider commitment to improving standards of attainment through a flexible and strategic use of the curriculum.

The policy of the North Lanarkshire Council is an outstanding example of promoting and supporting vocational studies as part of a strategy of "Raising achievement for all". Key features of the North Lanarkshire approach include validating the policy framework within which schools are willing to risk change, extensive consultation within schools, expert support for schools, an emphasis on flexibility and choice for students, and collaboration with external partners (colleges and industry) to deliver choice "on site" (North Lanarkshire Council 2004-2005, undated; Livingston, McCall and Seagraves, 2004).

The high level of student interest in vocational options as reported by North Lanarkshire schools points to the importance of engagement as a spring of achievement. There is a marked contrast between attitudes to the more traditional academic subjects and the newer vocational options (Livingston, McCall and Seagraves, 2004). Vocational options can work to increase motivation and partly address the problem of flagging interest in subjects of poorly perceived relevance (and higher examination risk).

International best practice

The North Lanarkshire model is not the only example of how vocational studies can restore student interest in their studies. An example of impacts observed in other national systems comes from a destinations tracking survey of approximately 34 000 young people completing their senior secondary certificate in Victoria in 2005. The Victorian Certificate of Education (VCE) offers students the facility of combining academic and nationally accredited vocational units. The latter are offered over a wide range of industry areas. Successful completion, based on assessed competency in each module, generates a national vocational award. Thus students obtain both the senior secondary certificate (VCE) and, within this, a national award under the Australian Qualifications Framework. Vocational studies were introduced partly to improve employability (as in Scotland), but their motivational affect has led to their increasing use in the lower forms of secondary school, beginning with 14 year-olds. Here there is no question of an early entry to work: the issue is how to get schoolwork done. From the school leaver survey of 2005, a comparison of views was made between those young people who included VET in their senior secondary programme and the weakest 25% of students in mainstream academic programmes who did not do VET. It was found that VET participants were more likely than low achievers taking only academic subjects to endorse the view that their study programme had been "satisfying and rewarding" (Teese 2007v).

A second example comes from New South Wales, where senior secondary students can also include vocational units in programmes qualifying for admission to university. Several large-scale longitudinal surveys of Higher School Certificate graduates have shown that, after controlling for achievement level, the morale, motivation and satisfaction of VET students is higher (Polesel *et al.*, 2007).

These two examples of the motivational impact of VET are drawn from one of Scotland's comparator nations. The curriculum in each of the jurisdictions mentioned is hierarchical and strongly focussed on competition for university places. The needs of low achievers have been overlooked in the past. VET has been introduced, not to serve this group uniquely, but to provide a new set of opportunities which are publicly valued (through national industry accreditation) and which have demonstrable economic benefits (including both employment and university transition). Experience since 1994 has shown that interest in VET is much wider and also that vocational studies lift student engagement. There is no evidence that aspirations for academic progression have been diminished. On the contrary, VET studies are recognized by Australian universities, and many VET students go directly to university on completion of their senior certificate. This is possible because academic and vocational subjects are nested within a single certificate which allows a balance of studies of more or less academic or vocational emphasis, while enjoying recognition from across different education and training sectors.

If vocational studies can boost student motivation, they can also contribute to pedagogical change in more academic areas through greater attention to issues of learning style and student meaning, as emphasized in vocational courses. For this to happen, the right policy settings have to be established in schools. Again the OECD review team was impressed by the approach in North Lanarkshire. A feature of the North Lanarkshire model which deserves special mention is the policy that, where possible, **all** students should have access to vocational options. Provision issues may impose selection and restrict access. But the policy position is that vocational options are relevant to all groups and are not to be used simply as a means of accommodating under-achievers on their way out of school.

Once this recognition has been established, it becomes possible to influence school culture more broadly. This includes using collaborative learning methods—again an approach widely adopted in North Lanarkshire schools—and putting a greater teaching emphasis on where knowledge leads, how it is applied, and what use it has in real-world settings. These are all issues identified in Scottish research—including the evaluation study in North Lanarkshire—which bedevil student learning. Many students see no relevance in modern languages and are negative to mathematics. These are two of the mainstays of the traditional academic curriculum in Scotland, but enjoy very low levels of student interest. Can we improve the situation by drawing more on the collaborative, applied and problem-based learning approaches which the lowly status of VET has allowed it to develop? And if these approaches do improve quality of learning, greater conceptual mastery and more self-directed, self-paced learning for low achievers, shouldn't they be available to high achievers as well?

Barriers to change

In Scotland, the national debate highlighted the need to bridge the academic and vocational divide. While impressive efforts are being made in some schools to do this, the overall picture is that Scotland is lagging behind best practice in comparator nations and not necessarily learning from its own best practice. A number of constraining issues need to be addressed to move forward more boldly and more confidently. Unless these issues are addressed, the pursuit of a *Curriculum for Excellence* risks being held back or frustrated.

(a) the need for a broad policy on vocational studies

Issue no. 1 is the lack of a broad policy vision of the role of vocational studies in Scottish secondary schools. Why should schools offer vocational options, at what level, to whom, for what range of impacts, with what partners, within what framework of curriculum and qualifications? These questions go to the very heart of curriculum reform. Yet in the national curriculum development process, VET continues to be treated to one side.

The reviews of recent research conducted as part of the development of a *Curriculum for Excellence* have highlighted issues, such as learning environment, choice of teaching and learning approaches, the ways in which learning is organized, and teachers' "understandings, values and autonomy" (Christie and Boyd, undated), all of which can be informed by the experience of delivering VET, both in Scotland and internationally. But there appears to be a separation between the 'mainstream' development work for the new 3-18 curriculum, on the one hand, and the development of Skills for Work courses, on the other.

For example, the reviews just cited of research-based literature were conducted within the reference framework of the 5-14 curriculum. Vocational studies were not included, presumably because until very recently they were not offered by schools. Yet many OECD countries have experience in delivering vocational education and training programmes to students in junior secondary school, to say nothing of the experience in the further education sector in Scotland. Similarly, the small group consultations on different areas of the curriculum also stayed within the subject-area framework of the 5-14 guidelines. At the same time, a large number of national vocational courses were designed and piloted. These included Construction, Early Education and Childcare, Engineering Skills, Financial Services, Hairdressing, Health and Social Care, Hospitality, Practical Experiences: Construction and Engineering, Rural Skills, and Sport and Recreation. All these courses are meant to help young people "develop a range of generic employability skills and abilities", and they are all seen as helping "candidates become successful learners, confident individuals, responsible citizens, and effective contributors" (SQA, 2006, p. 5). But are the designs of these courses based on the principles of the incoming 3-18 curriculum, and is the experience of implementing them contributing to the design of other courses that are 'mainstream' and not vocational?

Will it be possible to bridge the academic and vocational divide if developmental work proceeds independently, even when there is cross-referencing across areas of the old curriculum? Will it be possible to achieve one of the major objectives of a *Curriculum for Excellence*—a "single coherent curriculum for all young people"?

One of the concerns of the OECD review team is that the design of the 3-18 curriculum should draw fully on the experience of delivering vocational education and training to young people, both in Scotland and internationally. What can be learnt that is of potentially general application from models of applied learning, problem-based learning, collaborative learning, and structured enterprise- or community-based work placements? Can knowledge gained from these contexts help design 'mainstream' programmes with a view to improving student engagement and achievement?

Another concern is whether the new national courses in Skills for Work are applying the design principles of a *Curriculum for Excellence*, so that these courses do have the breadth of purpose that national curriculum reform envisages? Or are they more narrowly focussed on employability?

Again, what is the planned integration of student learning across vocational courses, on the one side, and academic or general courses, on the other? For example, how does a student who studies science and engineering go from practice to theory, and vice versa? Will there be linkages between the learning acquired in one classroom or enterprise context and another context? This is one of the most important examples of the multi-disciplinary approach recommended by *A Curriculum for Excellence* (SEED, 2004, p. 13).

Establishing a broad policy vision for the role of vocational studies is important not only for applying a strong **pedagogical** emphasis to this area of the school curriculum (and indirectly to others as well), but creating the space to innovate more freely. Schools are accountable for their performance, and unless there is a national or at least a local authority mandate for initiatives in this area, there will be reluctance to move forward. This is borne out by the evaluation of North Lanarkshire school programmes. This reported the views of headteachers regarding the need for "protection" against adverse inspection in the absence of a clearly endorsed mandate for change (Livingston, McCall and Seagraves, 2004).

(b) the delivery of vocational studies

Issue no. 2 concerns how vocational education for school students is delivered. Can the academic and vocational divide be effectively bridged if schools 'farm out' Skills for Work courses to colleges? The best way of bridging this divide is to draw on the principles underlying applied learning to construct units of instruction in academic and general courses, and on the other hand to develop clear linkages between these courses (with their increasingly theoretical emphasis) and vocational studies. In other words, a student should be able to learn 'theoretical' subjects through practical problem-based learning (in addition to other approaches) and also be able to proceed from more practical subjects to more theoretical ones (*e.g.*, from electronics to sub-atomic physics).

Can this happen if academic and vocational courses are taught in two different environments, by differently trained staff (who may not share the same values or teaching styles), and for basically different reasons? The colleges place a strong emphasis on employability (though this is not narrowly conceived), while schools put their emphasis on preparation for further study (though again not narrowly). What is important about the academic and vocational divide is not only the risk to innovation, creativity and intellectual breadth that rigid divisions between subjects presents, but the social divide that these divisions come to translate. Bringing the academic and the vocational domains more closely together includes widening social access to the academic curriculum, while at the same time pursuing greater intellectual depth through more varied approaches to teaching and learning.

The experience of Scottish education is that high overall standards can be achieved, while reducing inequalities at the same time (*e.g.*, Paterson, 2001). With the Standard Grade reforms, a major step was taken in widening access to secondary education. But additional steps are now needed to improve quality of learning as the basis for higher levels of participation both in upper secondary and in tertiary education. These steps, envisaged by the Munn committee, require schools to diversify their programmes without segregating their pupils. This lies at the heart of comprehensive schooling and was confirmed by the National Debate. However, selective reliance on colleges works against this. It dulls the stimulus to curriculum renovation within schools by exporting the students whose needs most require curriculum reform. And it views the vocational subjects which are outsourced as largely for employability, not as vehicles of broader cognitive and personal growth. This approach seems, moreover, to work against the grain of the "single coherent curriculum for all young people aged 3-18", which is the aim of a *Curriculum for Excellence.*

(c) programme structure or modular flexibility?

Issue no. 3 relates to the sequencing or packaging of vocational options in student programmes. Skills for Work courses currently represent discrete elements which are combined with other Standard Grades, national courses or units at the discretion of the individual student within the context of what is available at school or by arrangement with a college. Unlike in countries such as Norway, Sweden, France or Australia, vocational courses do not form sequences or programmes of study. Group awards have not been popular, and the emphasis has been to prefer flexibility over structure. This preference runs the risk of incoherence, low prestige, and diminished impact. Flexibility is not necessarily an advantage to young people whose levels of achievement exclude them from the clearest and most secure passages through school to further education and work. In other areas of the curriculum, sequence and progression are major features, *e.g.*, in mathematics, science and languages. It ought to be possible for students to specialize to an extent in vocational areas within a broader framework to ensure balance, just as it is possible to specialize in academic areas. At present, young people in Scotland have to leave school in order to do this. This affects both the capacity of schools to offer vocational studies in the compulsory years—for staffing profile cannot be built on marginal choices—and the culture of the school more broadly.

It is instructive to consider the curriculum reform experience in some of the Nordic countries. In Finland, following the implementation of basic comprehensive schooling in the 1970s, upper secondary education was reformed and all vocational training was organized into broad programmes, requiring at least two years of study. Since the 1990s, all upper secondary courses of a vocational nature are three-year, full-time programmes, whose graduates also qualify for admission to tertiary education (Aho, Pitkänen and Sahlberg, 2006). In Norway, vocational studies are organized in nine different programmes. Most young people undertake a pattern of two years school-based VET, followed by a two year apprenticeship with a firm. There is also an option of completing three years of school-based VET. In addition, young people have the choice of electing to undertake academic studies on completion of their two-year vocational programme in order to qualify for admission to higher education (Helland, Lødding, Markussen *et al.*, 2006). In both Finland and Norway, vocational studies are offered as structured programmes rather than loose combinations of modules and units, whose cognitive value and economic impact may vary widely.

Were Scotland to follow the lead of some of its comparator nations, it would structure vocational options into programmes to span the compulsory and post-compulsory years. Its schools would offer structured pathways (which may link with college programmes) instead of unconnected courses or units which might be construed simply as exit visas. The OECD review team were advised in some schools that there was a need to offer Skills for Work courses in S3 and that students should have access to a suite of courses offered in subsequent stages. The sequencing of courses should ignore the current divide between "compulsory" and "post 16"—since over two-thirds of all students stay on—and follow the lead of schools offering national courses in place of Standard Grades. Constructing pathways should be a cross-provider responsibility, as it is in New Zealand, through programmes such as the National Curriculum Alignment project (TES 2007).

(d) examinations and qualifications

Issue no. 4 is about assessing and certifying student learning. The Scottish Credit and Qualifications Framework (SCQF) offers students considerable flexibility. But, as we have stated, its complexity is also strongly marked by successive reforms, the features of which have tended to be conserved and to accumulate over time. The foreign observer encounters various phases of Scottish education history in the SCQF and wonders how much of this history each new generation of young people really must be saddled with. If two out of three students stay on today (and over four in ten reach S6), Scotland still retains a system of Standard Grades examinations as if the great majority of young people leave school at the earliest possible age. More and more schools draw from the palette of national courses. Most young people expect to enter white-collar jobs, many of which require higher education. They back this by staying on at school, and the curriculum seeks to support them through differentiated qualification levels, so that even low achievers have a place.

By operating examinations at S4, Scotland retains a significant barrier to progression. This is because the hierarchy of numbers and levels of qualification effectively ranks all individuals and offers a guide as to whether an individual should stay on or leave. Examination grades encourage selection and offer institutional rewards to continue and institutional sanctions against continuing. Low achievement predicts failure, high achievement predicts success.

The gateway represented by Standard Grades introduces a break between the compulsory and the post-compulsory years and inhibits programme progression, though it does not stop student progression. The fit between courses in S3/S4 and those in S5 is far from perfect, and neither the differentiated structure of national courses nor the differentiated levels of Standard Grades overcomes this problem. Essentially students straddle two periods in Scottish history—not only of qualifications, but of participation in secondary school. Lack of clear programme progression frustrates weaker learners who are checked by the examinations in S4, even though opportunities have been created for them through the Higher Still reforms.

This is not a favourable context for the growth of vocational options in Scottish schools. Skills for Work courses are introduced at the end of a stage of schooling and with an eye largely to employability on leaving school. They are not introduced as part of a pathway leading to further study or training in the VET area or to support further study in an academic domain. The examinations tend to enforce a terminal perspective or at least to reinforce a view about VET studies as being for students leaving school.

However, there is also a problem of the pedagogical emphasis in S3/S4. This is on exam preparation and navigating a passage through the hierarchy of qualifications at this stage of schooling. Graded assessment involving examination norms dominates horizons. Vocational options stress what the learner can do ("competency") over how he or she compares with other learners ("rank"). This approach is penalized by an examination system, and it is not surprising that Scottish schools have been reluctant to embrace VET in the context and given their accountability. The use of examinations for S3/S4 students does not appear compatible with a wider and more strategic use of vocational studies aimed at improving engagement and achievement.

A future for Standard Grades?

The difficulties of introducing vocational studies into the curriculum points to a larger issue which we have raised. Why, when two-thirds of a cohort stay on at school, is a system of qualifications retained as if it were differences in these qualifications that were essential rather than quality of learning and the kinds of study that are subsequently attempted? It does seem as if schools are made to be more concerned with distinguishing between individuals at an assumed point of finality in schooling—now overtaken—than creating opportunities for young people to go beyond this point and undertake more demanding and enriching tasks, including in the workplace.

It might be argued that many young people continue to leave school at the minimum leaving age and must have a report to represent their achievements, however modest. This is true. But what is better—a reformed programme of studies that is seen as purposeful and meaningful and can aim at high accomplishment in a range of areas or a transcript of examination results which shows how little academic learning has occurred? For those young people who struggle with schoolwork, it is better that they have access to good quality programmes with inbuilt incentives to learn and with demonstrated practical outcomes than that they have a results sheet listing inferior numbers and levels of qualifications, as if these spoke eloquently on their behalf. The examinations do not work for them, and offer no guide as to what the young person may be able to do for others.

But nor it is clear that Standard Grade examinations work for average or high achievers. They often stay on at school, are sometimes shocked at the extra work that the exams did **not** prepare them for—which belies the "preparatory" rationale for exams—and in any case can take as many more exams as they like to speak for them later.

Conclusion

In this chapter, we have stressed the importance of curriculum reform as a vehicle for raising standards of achievement in line with the philosophy of a *Curriculum for Excellence*. This means tackling the barriers to achievement encountered by the weakest learners, while ensuring that the efforts of high achievers are properly supported. Earlier curriculum reform in Scotland was focussed on lifting levels of participation by adjusting academic demands. Today the concern has to be with translating participation into achievement. Earlier reform efforts differentiated examination levels to allow certification of achievement at different levels.

That has created space for new populations to complete school. But it has not created incentives to achieve well. The reforms of the 1980s saw the need for these incentives and wanted variation and flexibility in the curriculum. That has come lately and tentatively. Scotland's comparator nations have modernized their curricula through nationally accredited programmes of VET. In Scotland, Skills for Work courses are new and still at the edge of change. The lead given by enterprising local authorities, such as North Lanarkshire, is not yet reflected in a broader national understanding of the role and purpose of VET, which continues to be narrowly conceived. Moreover, the planning process for the new 3-18 curriculum does not seem connected with the rollout of Skills for Work courses. The potential of VET to have a wider influence on curriculum through its emphasis on applied, co-operative and problem-based learning is thus at risk of being ignored. But so, too, is the big lesson from VET. Students need meaning, incentives and purpose to work. Attention has also been drawn to issues concerning delivery of VET, which should be viewed in the context of school culture, not simply costs; program structure and progression over modular flexibility and uncertainty; and finally the constraining role and lack of clear purpose of Standard Grade examinations.

Our view is that vocational studies—if viewed broadly—are the most powerful vehicle for implementing a *Curriculum for Excellence*. This is because—if properly designed—they require a change in pedagogical emphasis and course design towards shared learning approaches, problem-solving, and applied learning. It is also because they combine intrinsic benefits (enjoyment of learning through meaning, purpose and support) and extrinsic ones (vocational skills, employability, wider transition options, including higher education). From this perspective, we see the future of curriculum reform in Scotland as requiring a major revaluation of and national investment in vocational studies.

However, this revaluation should be seen as only part of a wider effort to broaden and deepen the quality of educational experience of all young people in Scotland. Far-reaching changes are needed to realise the aspirations expressed in the National Debate and subsequently in the work of the Curriculum Review Group.

Firstly, an overhaul of examinations seems inevitable. Standard Grades seek to **conclude** a stage of schooling. But it is not summative finality that is needed at this late compulsory stage: it is preparation and pathways building. Standard Grades truncate the passage to a fuller educational experience instead of preparing for it. More clearly defined pathways are needed to support further learning in a range of contexts, not a gateway which for many young people ushers them out of further learning.

Secondly, the fragmentary nature of the qualifications based on examinations for national courses seems to be incompatible with the fundamental objectives of curriculum reform. The new 3-18 curriculum wants breadth of purpose and of educational experience in school programmes. This makes more demands on young people than they are currently exposed to in the post-compulsory years (and in settings outside school). In Scotland, students leave school with a very wide range of qualifications. There are no defined minimum standards and there is no concept of graduation from upper secondary school. So how is successful achievement of the four purposes of the 3-18 curriculum to be attested?

The commonality of eight Standard Grades to mark the conclusion of compulsory school has no parallel in the post-compulsory years, even though the stakes have been raised—not by statute, but by public expectation about the qualities of a well-educated young person. If all young people in Scotland are to become "successful learners, confident individuals, responsible citizens, and effective contributors", this implies (a) continuing and certified education and training effort beyond the compulsory years, in whatever context, and (b) a concept of completion or graduation which sets minimum standards and reflects the four purposes of the curriculum.

There will be different paths, and differences in the balance of studies—academic, vocational, employment-based, campus-based, full-time, part-time, graded assessment, competency-based assessment. The SCQF enables pathways to be designed that allow this diversity, while ensuring overall coherence and minimum standards. At the end, when public certification really is needed, all young people who do meet the minimum standards, by whatever regulated path they take, receive the one certificate, testifying to the breadth and depth of their educational experience.

References

Aho, E., Pitkänen, K., and Sahlberg, P. (2006), *Policy Development and Reform Principles of Basic and Secondary Education in Finland since 1968*. Education Working Paper, Series 2, World Bank, Washington.

Christie, D. and Boyd, B. (undated), *A Curriculum for Excellence: Overview of recent research-based literature*, University of Strathclyde. *http://www.curriculumforexcellencescotland.gov.uk/images/A%20Curriculum%20for%20Excellence%20Overview_tcm4-252167.pdf*

Helland, H., Lødding, B., Markussen, E., Sandberg, N. and Aasen, P. (2006), "Education and Training of 15-20 year-olds in Norway", paper presented at the second annual conference of the International Research Group on Youth Education and Training, Melbourne.

Livingston, K., McCall, J. and Seagraves, L. (2004), *Evaluation of the North Lanarkshire Curriculum Flexibility Project*, University of Strathclyde, Glasgow.

North Lanarkshire Council (2004-2005), *Standards and quality report 2004-2005: raising achievement for all.* North Lanarkshire Council, North Lanarkshire.

Paterson, L. (2001), "Education and inequality in Britain", paper prepared for the social policy section at the annual meeting of the British Association for the Advancement of Science, Glasgow, 4 September 2001. *http://www.institute-of-governance.org/onlinepub/paterson/educ_inequality.html*

Polesel, J. *et al.* (2007), *Career Moves. Destination and Satisfaction Survey of 2005 HSC VET Students in New South Wales*, NSW Department of Education and Training, Sydney.

SED (Scottish Education Department) (1977), *Assessment for All: Report of the Committee to review assessment in the third and fourth years of secondary education in Scotland (The Dunning report)*, Scottish Education Department, HMSO, Edinburgh.

SEED (Scottish Executive Education Department) (2004c), *A Curriculum for Excellence,* The Curriculum Review Group, Edinburgh.

SQA (Scottish Qualifications Authority) (2006), *Skills for Work courses: a review of the first year of the pilot*, SQA, Glasgow.

Teese, R. (2007v), Unpublished analysis (for source, see Teese *et al.*, 2007a)

TES (2007), Supporting the Monitoring and Evaluation of the Tertiary Education Strategy,http://wiki.tertiary.govt.nz/~TESMon/Main/HomePage

7. Going Forward

Scotland's schools have been under continual reform since the 1960s. Throughout the last half-century, they have been challenged again and again about how well they serve the children and young people they enrol, about the kinds of knowledge they transmit, and about the cultural and economic impact they make. Over time, the public scrutiny of Scottish schools has intensified and expectations have risen. More use has been made of schools and more reliance placed on them. All sections of the Scottish community have asked more of schools. Working-class families have seen many of their jobs disappear, leaving their children like economic refugees who have no choice but to succeed at school. Business and professional families have seen the advantages of social position weaken in favour of "achieved status", with success at school and university training the new key determinants. Within families, girls have overtaken boys in the use of school—having been more quickly excluded from the changing labour market—and boys can no longer take refuge from school in the labour market.

Efforts made on all sides to use school well have helped make Scotland's schools work well. They are worked as a community asset. Where aspirations and abilities most diverge, the comprehensive secondary school makes the same promise as the primary school: care for the whole child and for all children. The welcoming of children with special needs is as much a sign of openness as the determination of the poorest schools to have the most reluctant learners unfailingly attend. So, too, is the welcoming of younger and younger children in nursery classes, trusted to primary schools because they can be trusted to nurture them as children first.

If the people of Scotland now depend on education more than ever before, they still see schools as a community resource to be shared rather than worked to the advantage of the best placed individuals. They see quality as coming from the leadership of a school (at all levels), but exercised within a wider framework in which local communities have a voice. This enables schools to be operated as a system for sharing resources and experience, and to be supported in proportion to the tasks they perform within the system. Schools are well led and staffed to a high standard. The

Teachers' Agreement has infused new life into schools, and the training and induction of new teachers is world class as is the Scottish approach to the professional development of headteachers. All schools are regularly reviewed, and a culture of critical self-evaluation is growing which answers the central role which success at school now plays for everyone.

These strengths of Scotland's schools show in the consistently high performance of 15 year-olds in PISA. Few nations outperform Scotland in mathematics, reading and science, and there is less variation in mathematics performance than in any other country except Finland. The proportion of students achieving at low or very low levels is one of the smallest in the OECD.

But Scotland also faces challenges. The biggest challenge is to make its comprehensive secondary schools work consistently well and equitably. Little of the variation in student achievement in the country is due to differences between schools. Most is due to differences "within schools". In Scotland, who you are is far more important than what school you attend, and at present Scottish schools are not strong enough to ensure that "who you are" does not count.

Student differences in socio-economic status are the most important factor, accounting for 18% of variance in mathematics performance. There is a very large gap between young people in the bottom fourth band of socio-economic status and the top fourth band, with Scotland lagging considerably behind some of its comparator nations—the Netherlands, Korea, Canada and Finland. There is also a large gap in reading, with socio-economic status accounting for twice as much variation as in Korea, Canada and Finland.

Taken together, these findings suggest that young people from poorer backgrounds face significant barriers in accessing a system of high performing schools. Two points in this observation should be emphasized: (a) the schools are **high performing**, not mediocre; and (b) young people from "poorer backgrounds" represent a **large proportion** of the total population of children in Scottish schools—every third primary school child lives in poverty and every fifth secondary school student (The Poverty Site, 2007s).

The social divide in Scottish comprehensive schooling tends to be masked, not only by a high overall standard of student achievement, but by international comparisons of resource levels and school facilities. There is considerable **formal equity** in Scottish schools as judged by headteachers and on criteria such as student-teacher ratios, trained staff, specialist staff, and facilities and other physical resources. Moreover, the views of students taken as a whole are positive (and improving over time).

The achievement of formal equity in schools underlines the point that in Scotland, it is not wide qualitative differences between schools that is the problem, but the unequal openness or accessibility of **good schools** to young people from different social backgrounds. Comprehensive schooling favours equity, but does not guarantee it. This is not only because family economic and cultural factors weaken student aptitude and interest, but because there are cultural and organisational factors **within schools** that act as barriers. These factors are common to the culture and organisation of schools as a whole and do not differentiate between them. They thus appear to be neutral to schooling (small "between school" differences), though they are not socially neutral. These factors include curriculum and examinations, teacher values and expectations, teaching style, pupil grouping practices (*e.g.*, "setting"), and resource allocation practices (which students get which teachers?).

One symptom of the impact of these factors is the wide variation in student ranking of mathematics classes. Differences in disciplinary climate predict differences in achievement. In Scotland, the gap is the highest of its comparator nations, and the index of climate has three times the predictive power. Given the links between student achievement and socio-economic status, it is probable that the worst mathematics classes in Scotland are not randomly distributed across the country, but concentrated in urban areas where there is a big gap between curriculum and culture.

National data from tests and examinations confirm the strong linear relationship between attainment and socio-economic status and also the impact of social area deprivation. On the one hand, there is a common set of factors operating in good schools which weaken learning chances for children from low socio-economic status homes. On the other hand, there is a set of urban area processes of differentiation and partial segregation which intensify home disadvantage and weaken operating conditions in schools.

Without effective action to tackle both the environment of social deprivation and problems in the routine ways in which good schools work, other 'attainment-based' problems are likely to persist. These include a continuing, comparatively high proportion of young people classified as 'not in education, employment or training' (NEET), flat staying-on rates in secondary school, large differences in success rates in national qualifications, limited growth in transition to further education, and social inequalities in higher education.

The OECD review team wishes to stress the responsiveness of Scottish schools to the challenges they face. While we are unable to provide a detailed discussion of initiatives, it is important to note the many ways in which schools and their local authorities are working to effect change within the constraints of existing institutional arrangements. Below we have set out approaches that appear to be fruitful. Our recommendations seek to build on these, while also looking more broadly at institutional arrangements themselves.

Table 1 School-based changes to improve achievement and transition

1. Better communication with parents, but targeted and consistent, with more support and sharing between parents of information and skills (e.g., home-link workers, early intervention to improve skills of both staff and parents, regular group meetings with parents, automatic reporting of absences)

2. Greater oversight and more individual attention in the compulsory years (e.g., monitoring and tracking of student progress, identification of needs, individualized learning plans)

3. A concentration of experienced and innovative teachers in the compulsory years (including mentoring of newer staff)

4. Capacity-building with a strategic emphasis (prioritizing CPD to the School Development Plan, support for projects under Headship programmes)

5. Additional teaching support activities to manage transition (e.g., summer school for S3/S4)

6. More flexible approaches to teaching (e.g., team teaching, small group teaching)

7. Greater use of applied learning and shared tasks (e.g., collaborative learning, practical projects to build self-esteem and social cohesion)

8. A pedagogical emphasis on vocational studies (e.g., offering VET courses to all students, long-term retraining of staff to build capacity and change culture)

9. Economic incentives for student engagement through clearer links between school and work or further study (e.g., Skills for Work, Enterprise studies, business partnerships for apprenticeships and work experience)

10. More school-based provision of VET and more selective and strategic use of college links (e.g., major investment in industry-standard kitchens, teach-in agreements with colleges to change

attitudes in schools and gain economies of scale; collaboration between schools)

11. Wider consultation with students over quality of instructional experience (both teaching and study) (Student Evaluation of Learning software, surveys designed by schools themselves)

12. More choice by students, based on their perceived needs and priorities (e.g., voluntary participation in VET, but selection into programmes; full certification of attainment)

These approaches have helped guide our thinking about the best ways forward and have given us confidence that what we do recommend endorses or extends on good educational policy and practice in Scotland itself.

While not wishing to specify measures, the review team considers that to effectively tackle the environment of poverty and deprivation and to make good schools work more equitably, a set of five broadly-framed strategies are required:

– **National priorities funding through local government compacts**

– **Greater school autonomy in a local government framework**

– **A comprehensive, structured, and accessible curriculum**

– **Continuous review of curriculum and teaching**

– **Monitoring of student destinations.**

National priorities funding through local government compacts

Scotland's approach is to deliver school education through local government. But more needs to be done to establish clear national priorities as a framework for local government policy, on the one hand, and on the other hand, local authorities need greater flexibility in operating national policies to achieve positive outcomes for their communities. Devolving the locus of decision-making so that it is closer to local communities is widely-established practice in Europe, even though there are different models and different histories. We will make some suggestions below for achieving this balance between national priorities and local government. However, before doing so, it is important to stress that much is at stake in getting this balance right, given the seemingly intractable problems of poverty and the tendency for success and failure to become ingrained without a continuing monitoring, evaluation and reform effort.

Over 30% of children in Scottish primary schools live in poverty (as defined by eligibility for free school meals). However, there are very high relative concentrations of poverty in Scottish cities. In Glasgow, nearly 3 in 4 primary schools are in the highest band of poverty; over half of all primary schools in Dundee are in the same category as are over 40% of primary schools in Inverclyde (The Poverty Site, 2007s). Thus the "playing field" is far from level.

Child poverty has been falling in Scotland—from 30% of all children in the mid-1990s to 24% in 2004/05 (as measured by relative low income, OECD equivalisation, after-housing costs) (SE, 2006i, Table 11, p. 12). But the continuing high densities of poverty in Scottish primary schools place a heavy burden on their performance. This has not prevented significant improvements. For example, since the late 1990s, the number of pupils in poverty who fail to achieve Level B in writing has fallen from about 33% to about 18%. Gains have been less dramatic, but still impressive in reading and in mathematics (The Poverty Site, 2007).

To sustain this improving trend and to make further progress may require more concentrated efforts from funding authorities. Currently there are several avenues available to achieve a greater concentration of effort. The first relates to special programmes which offer selected schools supplementary funding. Up to 42 secondary schools (or about 10% of the total) receive or are intended to receive Schools of Ambition grants. This programme has innovation at its centre. To the OECD review team, this is the right emphasis. However, a number of aspects of this programme are a concern.

Schools that qualify for funding include a mix of (a) those facing severe challenges and (b) those that have "strong ideas for transformation and can set new standards of excellence" (SE, 2007f). This spread of eligibility requirements risks diluting the limited additional funds available for transforming schools with the greatest environmental disadvantages. Is the priority to improve school performance where this is most needed or to fund innovation wherever this seems most promising? Innovation is most needed in the most challenged schools, and the "strong ideas for transformation" that arise in other contexts may not readily translate to the contexts which must be transformed as a **national priority**.

This concern extends to the breadth of the criteria for successful funding bids. "The best ideas will be generated by schools, who know their own circumstances and know what they could do with extra support to make a difference. **Each school is different and will have a unique path to transformation and improvement**." (SE, 2007f, emphasis added). If schools were so different, the ideas that they generate would have no wider relevance or application. Scottish authorities need to set firmer expectations regarding the educational improvements that are wanted and how schools propose to achieve these with the help of extra resources. The Schools of Ambition programme is not clearly tied in with a nationally planned improvement in student outcomes in the most challenged regions of Scotland. What difference will it make to the nearly 1 in 2 children in Glasgow who are poor readers?

Without a national framework within which improvements in achievement can be pursued and the efforts of schools and local authorities can be supported, there is a risk that current patterns of under-achievement will become entrenched and that generations of children will miss out on the benefits of successful learning.

Schools serving deprived communities currently receive funding weighted to relative need. They may also receive direct and ring-fenced grants for particular programs. However, the funding situation is complex. There are multiple and temporary funding lines, and reverse transfers through productivity demands. There is no certainty in the funding, no continuity, improvisation rather than innovation, and uncertainty about impacts and value-for-money.

Currently the approach to "deprivation" in Scotland is of a compensatory nature. Additional support is provided to offset family and community problems, but expectations appear to be modest, there is only limited knowledge of "what works", and successful experience is not being harvested, even if it is circulated through professional development and inspection. Compensation is the wrong emphasis. Schools should be funded to innovate and to produce durable change. Moreover, this should be part of a national learning effort in which experience is tested and builds into knowledge on which all schools can draw, including beyond the borders of Scotland.

There are therefore several issues to be addressed—consolidating and targeting the resource effort, balancing flexibility with accountability, and getting the purpose right. These issues have to be addressed within the framework of local government through which school education is delivered in Scotland.

A policy instrument is needed which sets out expectations about what is to be achieved, distributes resources according to need, and allows the responsible authorities flexibility in how resources are used.

Recommendation 1. That the Scottish Government develop a national innovation plan to fund improvements in educational

opportunities and outcomes through negotiated agreements with local authorities ("national innovation agreements").

Recommendation 2. That funding for the current Schools of Ambition programme be applied in a more selective and targeted way through the national innovation plan.

National innovation agreements should describe the changes in opportunities for learning, in quality of school and instructional experience, and in post-school education, training and employment outcomes that each local authority proposes to achieve and the strategies through which these changes are to be achieved.

The national innovation plan should be a framework for setting national priorities, ensuring that resources are equitably distributed and targeted to need, and harvesting and sharing knowledge of the most effective approaches to widening opportunities and improving outcomes. The plan should not impose strategies or approaches, but ensure that local authorities have the freedom, the flexibility and the means to achieve changes, while being accountable for the quality and effectiveness of their actions.

National funding to tackle disadvantage in education is currently provided to schools through the medium of the core local government finance settlement. This comprises a block grant as well as a number of specific purpose grants. The block grant is allocated by relative need, involving variable criteria and a view of spending priorities. The Scottish Government does not have a direct say in how the block grant is spent by local authorities, but on the other hand prescribes the purposes of the specific grants (which represent less than 10% of the total settlement).

While this approach is formally equitable, it is input driven. The OECD review team did not see evidence of the impact of expenditure on student outcomes. While the need for flexibility in the budgets of local councils is understood, the way in which grants are made does need to be seen in the context of the severity and persistence of inequalities associated with deprivation. An inputs-driven approach may satisfy the criterion of formal equity—ensuring balance across different local authorities—but it is another matter whether, within local authorities, spending does reach the children who most need support and does produce intended benefits. In short, while local councils may receive a just allocation, do schools and students within schools also receive a just allocation, and does this work?

We consider that greater autonomy for local councils, while desirable to achieve responsiveness, effectiveness, and accessibility of government, should be balanced by national monitoring of educational expenditure and outcome patterns. The national government is responsible for ensuring not only that there is an equitable allocation of resources between local authorities, but that expenditure programmes within local authorities achieve the outcomes for which they are intended. This requires periodic assessment and the collection of data adequate for the purpose.

To work well as an instrument of strategic resource allocation, the national innovation plan assumes that Scottish authorities are able to measure targeted improvements in children's learning, not only across Scotland as a whole, but within the boundaries of local government. Periodic measurement will provide the negotiated agreements between the Scottish Government and local councils with a reliable basis of information about levels and gaps in student achievement. Schools themselves also need to be able to measure improvements, both at an individual and a sub-group level.

Recommendation 3. We recommend that the Scottish Survey of Achievement be extended to all children throughout Scotland as a basis for negotiating resource and outcome agreements with local authorities and to enable improvements in schools to be measured at an individual and sub-group level.

While the national innovation plan establishes a framework for pursuing improvement and ensuring equity across Scotland, it will have limited impact if it is not accompanied by improvements in areas of housing, employment, health, and community services. The need for whole-of-government approaches is an important theme in Scottish public policy, and has led to major initiatives by the Scottish authorities (see *More Choices, More Chances*, SE 2006n, for an overview) as well as a strong emphasis on joined-up services through local government. Schools, alone, cannot overcome the barriers to success represented by poverty and deprivation. So the wider concept of intervention in Scotland is essential if a national innovation plan in education is to work well.

Greater school autonomy in a local government framework

Strategic resource allocation through a national innovation plan requires local councils to establish their own priorities for their communities in terms of the range of educational opportunities they make available, other services they provide, student access to different learning opportunities, and learning and transition outcomes for children and young people. The OECD team was impressed by the quality of the documentation provided by the education departments of local councils, though in some respects (especially benchmarked results) it was more uneven. In the context of more devolved responsibilities, it will be important for local authorities to establish clearer views about the impacts they seek to make, about how these are measured, and about the strategies they employ to achieve good outcomes.

Recommendation 4. Accordingly, we recommend that each local authority develops a policy framework which defines the priority impacts it seeks to make under the national innovation plan, including targeted improvements in student opportunities and outcomes.

Recommendation 5. We recommend that where a local authority provides additional resources to schools for equity purposes, it should do so within the framework of the national innovation plan as a means of concentrating the total resources available to a school, consolidating funds to achieve more flexibility and reliability, and enhancing the ability of the authority to evaluate programme effectiveness.

Greater autonomy for local councils over how funds are spent will give them more flexibility, and this in turn should allow schools to exercise a greater degree of management autonomy in their turn. This is especially important in a context in which institutional arrangements place schools under continuous scrutiny, on the one hand, while on the other hand limiting their freedom of action in the areas of curriculum and examinations. It was frequently observed to the OECD review team that the national 5-14 curriculum was not a legal requirement, though contributions to the National Debate implied either that it was or that it was perceived as having prescriptive force. If the national curriculum is effectively prescriptive, then any weaknesses in the design of courses or in the required structure of programmes or in the ability of schools to resource classes properly will react adversely on students. If schools have only limited decision-making powers over what teachers are employed (as well as what subjects are taught), the situation becomes still more difficult. In these circumstances, the professionalism of headteachers and classroom teachers cannot fully develop and is diverted into compliance behaviour.

There is little point in having a world-class system of headship training and a world-class system of professional induction if the scope for managing resources and the scope for managing curriculum are too constrained.

Schools need flexibility both in the teaching resources available to them and in what programmes they offer. Greater management autonomy is needed in these two critical areas—the power to determine and differentiate the range of demands made on students through the curriculum and the power to determine and differentiate the mix of teachers responsible for expressing these demands and helping students satisfy them. However, in a public system of education in which funding is provided through local government, school management autonomy has to be conditional on sharing responsibility for the needs of the whole community and meeting agreed objectives.

Recommendation 6. We recommend that local authorities negotiate agreements with schools under which greater management autonomy in staffing and curriculum is established in return for progress on an agreed platform of improvement in learning opportunities and outcomes.

Problems of under-achievement, poor engagement in schoolwork, low aspirations, and inequalities in access to higher education cannot be overcome simply by improved financial arrangements or even a greater concentration of resources at particularly disadvantaged sites within the school system. The issues are more complex. As we have stressed, they involve the routine ways in which good schools work. To effect the cultural changes in schools needed to improve equity and quality requires devolving greater management responsibility to schools. At the same time, however, the institutional framework of curriculum, examinations, and qualifications needs to be made more flexible so that schools can effectively exercise greater management responsibilities and teachers can exercise greater professional responsibilities.

A comprehensive, structured and accessible curriculum

Past reforms in Scottish secondary school education have focussed on differentiating levels of "complexity" or cognitive demand to give a wider range of children opportunities to progress. Examinations are set at different levels, and classes may be "set" at different ability levels (*e.g.*, in mathematics). Against this approach of "vertical differentiation", comparatively little effort at a system level has until recently been invested in "lateral differentiation"—that is, varying the content of the curriculum and opening the way to different styles of teaching and learning based on this. The failure to pursue this approach cannot be laid at the feet of the Munn committee. For that committee also recommended broadening the curriculum and did not base the whole of the reforms it proposed on lowering the examinations platform (Gamoran, 1996).

(a) diversifying the curriculum

The concepts and design principles of a *Curriculum for Excellence* offer a broad framework within which local authorities and schools can create a range of learning opportunities that contain both intrinsic and extrinsic incentives for engagement. It should be the responsibility of local authorities to ensure that their communities have access to a wide range of programmes, involving different delivery platforms (school, college, workplace), flexible approaches, and sharing and collaboration amongst providers. Schools, for their part, are responsible for offering a broad curriculum and for differentiating this to address particular strengths and weaknesses.

Recommendation 7. We recommend that each local authority develop an explicit policy framework which contains a charter of learning opportunities—a commitment to provide a range of education and training places in a delivery configuration which best suits the circumstances and needs of its communities.

(b) the role of vocational studies

We have stressed the importance of the twin objectives underlying the new 3-18 curriculum—creating incentives and raising achievement through this. In our view, vocational courses offer the single most important, though not the only vector for curriculum change. However, vocational studies should be seen in much broader terms than employability. In this report, we have emphasised a wider view which sees VET as a set of studies involving practical and collaborative learning, problem-solving and "cognitive sharing", varied contexts of learning, and strong incentives for engagement both in style of learning and in the acquisition of valued skills and experience. Employability is important, but secondary to the cognitive and developmental impact on the learner, and employability is also viewed in the longer term.

The review team considers that, on the basis of both international and national evidence, important benefits can be gained where schools deliver vocational studies on site. These benefits relate to cultural and pedagogical change in schools as well as greater social inclusiveness.

Recommendation 8. We recommend that, as a matter of national policy, vocational courses be accessible to all young people in schools from S3, and that sequences of study be developed spanning the compulsory and post-compulsory years.

Recommendation 9. We recommend that the Scottish Government support school-based provision of vocational courses where local authorities seek to implement this model within the framework of the national innovation plan.

(c) defining pathways

Scottish educational reform has removed barriers to the curriculum, but not necessarily created incentives to master it. Incentives for study are of two kinds: intrinsic and extrinsic. The intrinsic incentives relate to the intellectual enjoyment and satisfaction produced by good teaching and well-designed learning tasks, and good feedback through formative assessment and individual attention. Where these incentives are strong, students rely less on extrinsic motivation. However, when purpose and relevance are unclear and when, in addition, teaching is dull or mechanical, the role of extrinsic incentives widens. These relate to the links that exist between success in studies and a valued job, career or education pathway. Strong extrinsic incentives may compensate for weak internal motivation, just as on the other hand high interest in a course stimulated by enthusiastic and illuminating teaching can override any requirement to see where a course might lead. It is then the journey, not the destination, that counts.

The academic emphasis in Scottish secondary schools does not create strong incentives for weaker learners. Standard Grades may ask less of them through "setting" and lower levels of "complexity" in examinations, but the economic incentives for engagement have until recently been rather weak. Vocational training lay beyond school, and to a large extent still does. Even national courses that are described as "vocational" are sometimes of a more general character, with no clear linkages to employment. Weaker learners are more exposed to problems of meaning and purpose in the curriculum and their need for external incentives is greater. For stronger learners, the pathways are clearer—university or college. With the destination assured (though by no means automatic), the journey of work can be undertaken with confidence. While every secondary school student in Scotland receives one-to-one careers advice, this cannot compensate for the absence of clear and reliable pathways.

The problem of uncertain pathways for weaker learners may be thought to be managed by the "flexibility" of national qualifications. Colleges put great store by flexibility as they have a different "institutional logic" (Raffe, Howieson and Tinklin, 2007). Individual experiences weigh heavily. Students differ widely. Their self-confidence, persistence, and organisational skills may be low, their interests changeable, their attitudes to study inconstant. They may need a lot of support, attend irregularly, fail to complete work. In these circumstances, the capacity to vary learning programmes, to take units rather than courses, to switch and change, is essential. Stronger students, on the other hand, want building blocks, progression strategies, access to higher qualifications. Flexibility serves them too.

Clearer pathways in school would make weaker learners less reliant on flexibility at the end of school. For greater certainty in the destination helps mobilize efforts to make and continue the journey. *A Curriculum for Excellence* aims at providing a "single coherent framework" for all students. Does a curriculum "cohere" because its elements are linked in a knowledge sense? Or does it hold together (cohere) because it leads somewhere and is seen to lead somewhere?

Recommendation 10. That each local authority establish a curriculum planning and pathways network which links schools, colleges and employer groups to assist in establishing a charter of learning opportunities and defining the pathways through school to further education, training and employment.

It could be argued that the biggest impediment to the formation of pathways spanning the compulsory and post-compulsory years is the operation of Standard Grades examinations. These have tended to block implementation of vocational courses in schools and to inhibit programme and pedagogical innovation more broadly. On the other hand, they do not appear to be playing a positive role in the certification of student achievement, either for weaker learners leaving school (who have only poorer qualifications to speak on their behalf) or for stronger students who are advancing to S5 and face another round of examinations.

Recommendation 11. We recommend that Standard Grades examinations be phased out as the new 3-18 curriculum is implemented and as clearer and more effective pathways are established for the whole range of young people.

Recommendation 12. We recommend that a Scottish Certificate of Education be developed to sanction completion of an approved programme of studies or training, whether in school, college or employment. This "graduation" certificate should have defined minimum requirements to reflect the purposes of the new 3-18 curriculum, but also substantial flexibility as to content, level and duration of studies to ensure accessibility.

Recommendation 13. We recommend that young people proceeding to S5 undertake a programme of studies with specified minimum standards leading to the award of a Scottish Certificate of Education at the end of that year or at the end of S6, depending on the individual study pattern.

Recommendation 14. We recommend that those young people who choose to leave at the end of compulsory school negotiate an individual plan for further education and training to be undertaken over the next

two years under supervision of an appropriate authority (*e.g.*, a college), and that, if specified minimum standards of achievement or competency are met, they be awarded a Scottish Certificate of Education.

Continuous review of curriculum and teaching

Constructing pathways through the curriculum extends the economic benefits of school to the whole range of students. But the courses that young people study are not only about economic benefits. Arguably the intellectual and cultural benefits of school are more valuable. This makes it so much more important that courses work well **pedagogically**, and that they are regularly evaluated from this angle. Some courses will have a fairly direct link to employment and careers. But many courses do not. Student engagement thus depends on the intrinsic interest they generate in the hands of a good teacher. This is especially the case in fields, like mathematics, which become increasingly abstract and in which there is a marked falling away in student enjoyment, as we have noted earlier in this report

Quality of teaching and good programme design are key elements. The things that matter to students are informed and interested teaching, clarity in explanations, individual attention, clear assessment tasks, and good feedback. But, in practice, students have very limited opportunities to express their views about whether these things are achieved. Some schools do survey their students, as the OECD review team found on several visits. HMIe conduct pre-visit surveys of students. A culture of self-evaluation would welcome opportunities for students to report on the quality of their instructional experience. Increasingly in institutions of higher learning, this is the case. But it should be even more often the case in schools, where the teaching relationship is more personal and the dependence of the pupil on the master is much greater.

Recommendation 15. We recommend that education authorities in Scotland examine current approaches to gathering student feedback on quality of teaching (*e.g.*, the Student Evaluation of Learning software) and that they work with teachers to gain wider acceptance of the most promising approaches.

How students experience a course in instructional terms extends beyond teaching to the disciplinary climate of the classroom itself, the achievement impact of which can be considerable (as reported in Chapter 3). Variations in disciplinary climate are associated with differences in average achievement, and they raise a question which goes beyond the capacity of an individual teacher or the attitudes and behaviour of classmates. How robust is the design of a course from a teaching perspective, given the wide range of settings in which a course is delivered?

An SQA course can be regarded as a product put on the market for schools and colleges to deliver. Inputs to the design of the product are made by different professional and industry groups as well as institutions, including notably institutions that do not deliver the product and have no connection with the 'consumers' (either teachers or students), even while exercising very considerable influence over design. How good is the product? This depends on the institutional perspective. Universities want fitness for purpose (preparation, student ranking and selection). But from a teacher's perspective, what matters is whether a course that is potentially good and appropriate can be delivered well to his or her students. Overall, a course may work well in preparing a mass of students to undertake university studies, say in engineering or history. But how well does it work at the many different sites, urban and rural, rich and poor, that make up a school system? Can a course be taught widely and well? Or is it a case of "who you are" determining what you can study, or even "what school you attend" deciding the question?

The SQA does not currently have a perspective on where its many courses lead, but nor does it appear to have a perspective on how well its courses work in teaching terms. A study of social and gender patterns in course participation and success would shed light on this (*e.g.*, Croxford, 1997). But this would be from a student outcomes perspective. Over time, teachers in many different schools need to be consulted about their experience in the classroom in order to test the **pedagogical** strength of a course. No doubt this presents a complex challenge: what is due to a teacher, to design, to students? But each SQA course is a set of authoritative demands on student learning articulated by classroom teachers and applied in examinations. The formulation of these demands cannot ignore the variable capacity of students to respond or teachers to express and enforce demands. Many Scottish students find the transition to Highers a cultural shock, and this may be more marked in some courses than others, as S6 students informed the OECD review team. How can this problem be managed without consulting teachers about the demands that a course imposes? The shock may be such that a disproportionate share of total teaching resources is required to support upper secondary students, drawing away expertise and experience from weaker students in the compulsory years.

Recommendation 16. We recommend that rolling consultations be undertaken with teachers from a wide cross-section of schools regarding their classroom experience in delivering selected courses, the quality of course design, and learning outcomes for students.

Monitoring school leaver destinations

In much of our discussion so far, we have focussed on the structure of opportunities and the incentives, both extrinsic and intrinsic, for students to exploit these opportunities. If the test of intrinsic incentives lies in student evaluations of teaching, the test of extrinsic incentives lies in the destinations of students. The economic benefits represented by skills (generic and specific), practical experience, qualifications, and access to further education, training and employment have to be demonstrable, and not only for the average young person leaving school, but for defined sub-groups.

(a) longitudinal studies

Monitoring of school leaver destinations is a long-established part of theoretical and policy research in Scottish education. The panel studies conducted by the Scottish Survey of School Leavers (SSLS) are of international significance and influence. It is through them that progress in standards and in equity has been measured, thus creating a framework within which the impacts of policy can be assessed. This extends to international comparisons, including between Scotland and the rest of the United Kingdom. Related to this facility, which is a major benefit, is the theoretical work which SSLS is able to support. While there are other valuable sources of information on school leaver transition—notably from Careers Scotland—the key questions that policy-makers have to address require data on the "journey" as well as the "destination".

It is not enough to know the range of destinations reached by school leavers taken as a group. We have stressed in this report that in Scotland "who you are" matters as far as success at school is concerned. It matters just as much "how" you reached your destination—the processes and factors which raise or lower the chances of reaching a given destination. These matter because the greatest challenge facing teachers is to relate freely to the individual child and to remove all barriers to that child relating freely to the task. Without studying the journey, we cannot identify the barriers, the hazards thrown across the route, the signposts, sure or faulty, clear or misleading, and the baggage that has been carried from early in the trip or acquired along the way. Policy-makers are expected to make a difference. That means understanding the processes that make a difference. And that requires a video, not a snapshot.

However, the Scottish Survey of School Leavers in its current form has limitations. Greater depth of insight would be gained by making contact with young people before they leave school. Data should be collected on achievement level, quality of instructional experience, satisfaction with school, rapport with teachers and peers, academic self-esteem, and aspirations. It is important to use the survey to illuminate more of the school-level processes that affect school leaver destinations. To contain costs, it may be necessary to vary the scope of the survey in different years, with greater emphasis in some years on the antecedents of educational success and failure, and more emphasis in other years on post-school destinations.

Recommendation 17. We recommend that consideration be given to extending the scope of the Scottish Survey of School Leavers to make contact with young people well before they leave school and to provide fuller information about school achievement and experience.

(b) point-in-time studies

The SSLS offers a process-oriented analysis of student trajectories. This provides a system-wide perspective on 'who gets what, when and how?' This is the perspective of the policy-maker at a national level. But good information on student destinations is needed by schools and local authorities. This is provided by Careers Scotland. High schools need to know what happens to their students and to **all** of their students. This is above all to help them plan and evaluate curriculum. In this report, we have stressed the importance of creating or reinforcing the economic incentives for student engagement and achievement.

Schools do not control labour markets. But they do influence the employment aspirations and the competitiveness of young people entering the labour market, either directly on leaving school or after further study. Scottish high schools are comprehensive. This should imply, not only open intakes of young people (non-selectiveness), but breadth of curriculum, choice for students, and support for the full range of post-school destinations. This requires having a full picture of what happens to all individuals, including differences on key dimensions, such as achievement level and gender (and perhaps, also, depending on the context, ethnicity/language background). Each high school should be able to examine how well its programmes of studies work for high, average and low achievers, and separately for girls and boys, and by ethnicity/language background, where numbers allow.

Amongst Scotland's comparator nations, Australia has implemented comprehensive destinations tracking programmes in four of its States. In Victoria, where these programmes began, and which has a population about the size of Scotland's, all school leavers are contacted each year by a telephone survey. Individual reports are prepared for nearly 500 schools in the year of the survey. The brief, four-minute interview, does not yield information of the depth available to the SSLS. But it does allow every school to see what happens, not only to the whole cohort of exit students, but to sub-groups as well, *e.g.*, low achieving girls, high achieving boys, girls from lower socio-economic status backgrounds, etc. (depending on the size of the cohort). It is thus possible for schools to test how well the transition process works for all or most individuals and for whom it works less well. At the same time, the telephone contact with exit students ensures that post-school counselling can be offered to individuals in problematic transition (part-time or unemployed workers not in education or training) (see Teese *et al.*, 2007a; for school tables, Teese *et al.*, 2007b).

Recommendation 18. **We recommend that Careers Scotland investigate approaches to providing all schools and local authorities with comprehensive point-in-time data on school destinations, including work and study status, jobs, and hours of work, and broken out by qualification level and gender (at a minimum).**

Conclusion

The recommendations set out in this chapter are intended to achieve greater equity and effectiveness through five broad strategies—national priorities funding through local government compacts; greater school autonomy in a local government context; a comprehensive, structured, and accessible curriculum; continuous review of curriculum and teaching; and monitoring of school leaver destinations.

These are distinct, but related strategies which will support the current policy reliance on general measures of school improvement, formal equity of provision, marginal relative funding for deprivation, and quality assurance through local authorities and independent inspection.

Above all, these five strategies will help mobilize and impart a fuller sense of purpose and direction to a teaching force, now better recognized and supported than in the past, which has proved its effectiveness in high international standards of student achievement and improving national trends. As many new, enthusiastic and highly regarded teachers join the service, it is right to raise expectations, while setting these within a clear strategic framework, perhaps under the motto, *No equity without quality.*

References

Croxford, L. (1997), "The shape of the secondary school curriculum", *SCRE Newsletter*, Scottish Council for Research in Education, Glasgow.

Gamoran, A. (1996), "Curriculum standardization and equality of opportunity in Scottish secondary education, 1984-1990", *Sociology of Education,* No. 69, pp. 1-21.

Raffe, D., Howieson, C., and T. Tinklin, (2007), "The impact of a unified curriculum and qualifications system: the Higher Still reform of post-16 education in Scotland", *British Educational Research Journal*, Vol. 33 (in press).

SE (Scottish Executive) (2006i), *Statistics Publication Notice - Economy Series: Scottish Households Below Average Income 2004/05*, Scottish Executive, Edinburgh.

SE (Scottish Executive) (2006n), *More Choices, More Chances: A Strategy to Reduce the Proportion of Young People not in Education, Employment or Training in Scotland,* Scottish Executive, Edinburgh.

SE (Scottish Executive) (2007f), "News: Schools of Ambition", *http://www.scotland.gov.uk/News/News-Extras/schoolsambition* (29 July 2007)

Teese, R., *et al.* (2007a), *The Destinations of School Leavers in Victoria.* Department of Education and Early Childhood Development, Melbourne.

Teese, R., *et al.* (2007b), *2007 On Track Publication Data (by school).* Department of Education and Early Childhood Development, Melbourne.

The Poverty Site website (2007), "Educational attainment at age 11", *http://www.poverty.org.uk/S14/index.shtml*

The Poverty Site website (2007s), "Scotland: Concentrations of Poverty", *http://www.poverty.org.uk/S10a/index.shtml*

Annex 1. Terms of Reference for the Review of Education in Scotland

The National Policy Context

On 1 July 1999 a new Parliament and Executive were established in Scotland with legislative and executive responsibility respectively for a wide range of matters devolved from the UK Government, including education, training and lifelong learning. Scotland remains a full part of the United Kingdom and reserved matters *e.g.* foreign policy, defence, UK fiscal, economic and monetary matters continue to be governed at a UK level.

The First Minister for Scotland is responsible to the Scottish Parliament for the overall supervision and development of the education system in Scotland and for legislation affecting Scottish education, through The Scottish Executive Education Department (SEED) and Scottish Executive Enterprise, Transport & Lifelong Learning Department (SEETLLD). In practice, the First Minister delegates responsibility to the Minister (and Deputy Minister) for Education & Young People and the Minister (and Deputy Minister) for Enterprise & Lifelong Learning.

SEED has responsibility for pre-school and compulsory and post-compulsory school education. It broadly determines national aims and standards, formulates national policy, commissions policy-related research and analysis, provides a national programme of inspection, issues guidelines on curriculum and assessment and oversees teacher training and supply. SEETLLD has responsibility for post-school education, including lifelong learning, further and higher education, skills, employability and training.

Five National Priorities were approved by the Scottish Parliament in December 2000 under the Standards in Scotland's Schools etc Act. These were an expression of the high level priorities for the partnership government and have directed education policy developments since then. The 5 Priorities are:

- Achievement and Attainment

- Framework for Learning

- Inclusion and Equality

- Values and Citizenship

- Learning for Life

In November 2004 SEED published *Ambitious, Excellent Schools*[5], its agenda for action to modernise many aspects of Scottish education in pursuit of the broad aims of heightened expectations, stronger leadership and ambition; more freedom for teachers and schools; greater choice and opportunity for pupils; better support for learning; and tougher, more intelligent accountabilities. *Ambitious, Excellent Schools* contained 69 separate commitments under these five broad headings. By November 2005, a Progress Report[6] demonstrated that 38 of these had been achieved and work is currently taking place to achieve the remaining commitments.

An important element of *Ambitious, Excellent Schools* is the wide-ranging programme of work being taken forward under the title *A Curriculum for Excellence*. This programme of work is designed to produce a curriculum framework which will enable all young people from 3-18 to develop capacities as successful learners, confident individuals, responsible citizens and effective contributors. The Programme represents a major move towards an outcome-based curriculum. It will impact on all aspects of school education, including the design of the curriculum itself; teachers' development; elements of the qualifications structure; assessment methodologies; school and authority improvement planning; inspection; school buildings policy; linkages with the Further Education sector; preparing young people to enter education employment and training; and leadership, management and ethos within schools.

Key Ministerial priorities currently centre around implementing *A Curriculum for Excellence*; reforming assessment, including greater recognition of wider achievement; developing excellence within the teaching profession; improving leadership; breaking the link between deprivation and low achievement and attainment; attainment of looked after children; raising attainment and achievement and tackling the NEET[7] issue – in short, providing the right educational environment and opportunities to

---

[5]   Available at http://www.scotland.gov.uk/Publications/2004/11/20176/45852

[6]   Ambitious Excellent Schools Progress Report 2006

[7]   Young People aged 16-19 Not in Education, Employment or Training

achieve maximum potential for all learners, practitioners and leaders within the education system.

Purpose of Review

The economic, cultural, and social dimensions of globalisation and the emergence of the knowledge society intensify the pressure on governments and education systems everywhere to improve their quality, efficiency and equity.

Scotland performed well in both PISA 2000 and 2003, being ranked in the top third of OECD nations in all three literacies, and the system consistently delivers positive outcomes for a large majority of young people, with 79% of primary pupils (updated figure to come) reaching expected standards in 2003/04, and 59% of school leavers currently entering higher education at degree level cf. an OECD average of 53%.

In order to increase further the competitiveness and standing of its education system in the increasingly demanding European and global environment, and in line with the commitment made in *Ambitious, Excellent Schools* (2004) to benchmark Scotland against international standards as a basis for bringing about further improvement in performance, the Scottish Executive has asked the OECD to undertake a review of education in Scotland. The review will compare the performance of Scottish education to that of other OECD countries in order to assess its strengths and challenges, and to explore approaches which might add to our agenda in overcoming such challenges, and further reinforce strengths and improve performance. The increasing availability of internationally comparable data has provided additional impetus and means for doing so.

The Scottish Executive's key objectives for the review are:

- To invite the OECD to carry out a review of the quality and equity of education outcomes in Scotland.

- To structure the review in a way which integrates lessons from PISA and other benchmarking countries/regions with an expert analysis of key aspects of education policy in Scotland.

- To invite the OECD, on the basis of their analysis, to highlight areas of policy and levers which might add further value to our agenda of improving education outcomes for young people in Scotland.

Scope

Focusing principally on school education and the important transitions to and from this, it is intended to provide insights, informed by experience in other countries, into possible explanations for the observed outcomes; and to highlight policy directions that reflect international experience and good practice.

More particularly, the review will address key areas such as consistency of education outcomes across the country; equity of outcomes for young people from differing social backgrounds and personal circumstances *e.g.* looked after children, young people with additional support needs; and performance of the lowest attaining young people relative to other learners. It will also look at issues such as leadership, disengagement from learning and transitions across sectors, and consider where the key levers for positive change are in order to ensure that all young people are able to achieve their full potential.

Specific Questions to be Addressed

1. Viewed from an international perspective, what are the strengths and weaknesses of education in Scotland, particularly with reference to those who are not achieving their full potential, including those at risk of becoming part of the NEET group.

2. Do the range of current reforms, including specifically work in progress on the wider agenda of A Curriculum for Excellence, address the challenges sufficiently? How well do the reforms compare with reforms in countries which have common issues to deal with? How effective have implementation policies, particularly in respect of outcome-based curriculum reforms, been in comparator nations?

3. Are there international insights in the delivery of education to young people at risk of underachieving from which Scotland might draw? If so, what appear to be the principal benefits and advantages of these approaches to Scotland? And what are the most plausible strategies to deploy in a manner that respects the culture, values, and traditions of Scottish education?

4. How well do current reforms disseminate to the classroom? How effective are they at changing behaviour on the ground? Are the key messages being communicated effectively and getting through the system?

5. How sustainable is the current direction of travel?

Process

The OECD will use their customary format of 'peer review', carried out within the framework of reviews of national policies for education. This has been the mainstay of OECD comparative analysis work on education systems, utilising PISA results as a valuable tool in this respect which permits the analysis of performance outcomes. The review will combine a qualitative, expert-based approach with the quantitative analyses permitted through PISA data.

Schedule

Agree terms of reference	end November 2006
Agree scope and structure of background report	end November 2006
Complete background report	end February 2007
Visit by examiners	March 2007
Draft report	end September 2007
Special Session of OECD Education Committee and publication of final report	early December 2007

Annex 2. Programme for the Visit to Scotland by OECD Review Team, 12-22 March 2007

Organisations, institutions and stakeholders participating in meetings and seminars held with the OECD Examiners during their visit to Scotland, 12-22 March 2007

- Scottish Government Ministers and officials
- Her Majesty's Inspectorate of Education (HMIE)
- Learning and Teaching Scotland (LTS),
- Scottish Qualifications Authority (SQA)
- Convention of Scottish Local Authorities (COSLA)
- Educational Institute of Scotland (EIS)
- Association of Headteachers and Deputes in Scotland (ADHS)
- General Teaching Council of Scotland (GTCS)
- Headteachers' Association of Scotland (HAS)
- Scottish Secondary Teachers Association (SSTA)
- Scottish Borders – Local Authority, Westruther Primary School (Headteacher, teachers, students), Earlston High School (Headteacher, teachers, students)
- Inverclyde – Local Authority, Ravenscraig Primary School (panel of primary school Headteachers), St. Columba's High School (Headteacher, senior managers, students)
- Stirling – Local Authority, Bannockburn Primary (Headteacher and students), Brannockburn High School (Headteacher, senior managers, students)
- North Lanarkshire – Local Authority, St. Andrew's Primary School, Cardinal Newman High School, St Margaret's High School, Fallside Secondary (Headteachers, senior managers, students)
- Headteachers, Teachers, Students
- Researchers
- Careers Scotland

Representatives at GTCS seminar:
- GTCS
- Universities / Teacher Education Institutions
- Local Authorities
- CPD Team
- Probationers
- Teachers – Professional Recognition
- Chartered Teachers
- Scottish Qualification for Headship
- Teacher Organisations / Unions

Representatives at Closing the Opportunity Gap: Low Attainment and NEET Seminar - Scottish Government, SQA, Education Authorities, Scotland's Colleges, Universities, Headteachers, the Voluntary Sector, Employers and alternative providers of education.

Annex 3. The OECD Review Team

Richard Teese (rapporteur) is Professor and Director of the Centre for Post-Compulsory Education and Lifelong Learning in the University of Melbourne.

Simo Juva is Director of Education and Culture in the City of Lohja, Finland.

Frances Kelly is the New Zealand Ministry of Education's Education Counsellor in Europe.

Dirk Van Damme is Director of the Cabinet of the Flemish Minister of Work, Education and Training, and professor of educational sciences in Ghent University.

****

Gregory Wurzburg is a Senior Analyst in the Education and Training Policy Division, Directorate for Education, Organisation for Economic Co-operation and Development, Paris.

Karin Zimmer is a Senior Analyst in the Indicators and Analysis Division, Directorate for Education, Organisation for Economic Co-operation and Development, Paris.

OECD PUBLICATIONS, 2, rue André-Pascal, 75775 PARIS CEDEX 16
PRINTED IN FRANCE
(91 2007 21 1 P) ISBN 978-92-64-04099-1– No. 55967 2007

Printed in the United Kingdom
by Lightning Source UK Ltd.
135750UK00001B/215/P